Thomas Merton
A Bibliography

Books by Frank Dell'Isola

Thomas Merton: A Bibliography (Published by Farrar, Straus, and Cudahy, Copyright 1956 by Frank Dell'Isola)

The God-Man Jesus

The Old Testament for Everyman

Thomas Merton: A Bibliography (Published by The Kent State University Press, Copyright 1975 by Frank Dell'Isola)

Thomas Merton

A Bibliography

By Frank Dell'Isola

The Kent State University Press

The Serif Series: Number 31
Bibliographies and Checklists
William White, General Editor
Oakland University, Rochester, Mich.

Library of Congress Cataloging in Publication Data

Dell'Isola, Frank.
   Thomas Merton; a bibliography.
   (The Serif series: bibliographies and checklists, no. 31)
    1. Merton, Thomas, 1915-1968—Bibliography.   I. Series.
Z8570.6.D4   1975   016.2   74-79148
ISBN 0-87338-156-4

To Gretchen
who made the impossible possible

Contents

Introduction to the First Revised and Expanded Edition

Compiling this book was a tremendous labor of love. It was also a most difficult project to complete; Father Louis Merton was a dear and devoted friend. I first met him in 1955 at the monastery of Our Lady of Gethsemani in Trappist, Kentucky, where he slowly matured, wrote, lectured and taught the young seminarians, and lived as a Cistercian monk of the Order of Strict Observance; the purpose of my visit was to do the final research for a Thomas Merton bibliography which was later brought out by Farrar, Straus and Cudahy. Permit me to quote a brief passage from an article of mine, *A Journey to Gethsemani*, which was published in *Cross & Crown* (September, 1956). I would like to share my initial impression of the late Tom Merton.

"In a matter of minutes Father Louis visits me. Though this is our first meeting, I feel like I have known him for years. He has a contagious smile and humor; he still is Thomas Merton. I doubt very much if he will ever lose any trace of it. It would be a shame if he ever did. Meeting the man for the first time is an experience. He quickly puts you at ease; there isn't anything pompous, artificial, or affectatious in his demeanor. He talks and smiles like a small boy, but there is fire and determination in his words and actions. Yet his simplicity is overwhelming. These conflicting traits are in proper balance, and his happiness seems boundless."

Since then our friendship has grown and his last letter which arrived two weeks before his death was a note that touched me deeply.

It wasn't until three years after Merton's tragic and untimely demise that I decided to update and expand the Thomas Merton bibliography. Basically, the format and description of items adheres to the First Edition; the exception being parts "D" and "I" which have been omitted in the present work. In the earlier bibliography these sections read: "D: Critical Articles and Letters about Thomas Merton in Periodicals, Newspapers and Books," and "I: The Unpublished Works of Thomas Merton."

As indicated in the Introductory Note to the First Edition, only the American First Editions of Thomas Merton are described in detail, except the English and French entries, and the privately printed books of the late Thomas Merton in section "E" which are bibliographically significant.

There was much difficulty in tracking down many obscure publications: I could not locate the magazines, *Don Quixote* (only two issues were brought out), and the Italian *Convivium* which is published in Rome, Italy. Nor was I able to find the following periodicals: *Gnomon, American Dialog, Latitudes,* and *Freelance*; nor did I have any luck in finding a copy of "What Think You of Carmel?" I believe it was a pamphlet or paper-back.

It should be stressed that this is not a definitive bibliography of Thomas Merton. The late Father Louis was a prolific writer and at his death he left a mountain of notebooks and manuscripts which would ultimately fill at least two dozen books; these may, or may not, be published. Added to his literary stockpile, which is controlled by The Trustees of the Merton Legacy Trust, are the hundreds of unpublished collected essays, lectures, plus scores of mimeographed volumes which were written while he was Master of the Scholastics (1950 to 1954). Some of these items are described in detail in the 1956 version of the Merton bibliography, Section "I", pp. 79-84.

Numerous individuals and organizations have rendered invaluable service in the gathering and preparing of the hundreds of items that form the Merton bibliography but the responsibility for errors and omissions is entirely mine.

Special thanks are due to the staffs of the following college libraries: Woodstock and Saint Francis, for bringing many elusive items to my attention; to H. George Fletcher, Director of Fordham University Press, for his help and guidance through many difficult periods; to the kindly and helpful staff of the Rare Book Department of The New York Public Library, for the privilege of handling and examining the privately printed books of Thomas Merton; to Else Albrecht-Carrie, of New Directions, for her efficient and prompt help whenever called upon; to the staffs of Union Theological Seminary, Catholic University in Washington, the Library of Congress, Bellarmine College in Louisville, for their generous loan of materials; to Brothers Patrick Hart and Kevin White, for their overwhelming interest and sending along numerous items which I could not obtain anywhere; to Robert Wilson, of the Phoenix Book Shop in New York City, for his kindness in letting me browse through his huge collection of periodicals; to the very kindly staff of the Schomburg Center For Research in Black Culture, of The New York Public Library, for bringing certain rare items to my attention; and to Mrs. Irene Stoess, of UNESCO House, in Paris, for sending xerox copies of the bibliographical cards in volume 24 of *Index Translationum*.

And of course, I must single out my wife Gretchen, for her dedication and willingness to help when conditions seemed insurmountable due to illness; her endurance in caring for my needs, the reading and correcting of each section, showed a strength that was beyond exhaustion. This book could not be a reality but for her courageous spirit and loyalty.

F. D.

Introductory Note to the First Edition

This bibliography is an expanded and revised version of an earlier work of mine, *A Bibliography of Thomas Merton*, which was published in *Thought*.*

In compiling this initial bibliography of Thomas Merton, the descriptive method used in listing his American First Editions is similar to the form adopted by the American Library Association and used in the cards printed and distributed by the Library of Congress. I have taken certain liberties with the standard procedure of listing which wholly ignores blank leaves and unnumbered printed preliminary leaves, in order to account for all leaves, either those upon which any printing appears, or blanks, or end-papers, the better to establish the priority of a First Edition.

Only the American First Editions of Thomas Merton are described in detail, except the two English entries in section "F" which are bibliographically significant. Later editions and impressions are wholly ignored except those of bibliographical import.

The index pattern does not adhere to a unified alphabetical sequence. For ease and immediate reference it has been divided into nine separate sections, i.e., Book Index, Index of Merton Articles, Index of Articles about Merton, Poetry Index, Index of

---

* *Fordham University Quarterly*, XXIX, 115 (Winter, 1954-55), [574]-96.

Foreign Publications, Index of Translators, Index of
Unpublished Items, etc., Index of Juvenilia, Index of Names.

All books, pamphlets, newspapers, periodicals and records
described and noted herein have been personally examined by
me (except where indicated) and form a part of my library.
Definitiveness has been my constant objective but a bibliography,
however comprehensive it purports to be, can never be
complete while the author is still engaged in writing.

Mention here should be made of two rare items of Merton's
which were published in England in 1930, when he was fifteen.
An essay entitled "Titus Oaks" was published in the Grantham
Journal and another entitled "A Famous Old Oakhamian"
was published in the Lincoln, Ruthland and Stamford *Mercury*.
Correspondence to these newspapers has brought no response.

From Father Louis I have learned that parts of *Seeds of
Contemplation* appeared in Polish behind the Iron Curtain and
excerpts translated into Czech have been published in England;
I have seen neither. Merton also wrote the text and prayers
for two prayer-cards (one for the Feast of Saint Joachim, and
the other for the centenary celebration of the founding of
Gethsemani) which were published at Gethsemani (no longer
available; I have not seen them). Finally, Father Louis was
also responsible for a piece, "The Man of Great Possessions,"
which may have appeared in Friendship House *News* (1941 or
1942); I could not track this down. This magazine also
reprinted a poem, "Holy Communion: The City," which I was
unable to locate. There is also an article, "Il Papa Della
Madonna," which Merton wrote for inclusion in a commem-
orative volume given to Pius XII on his 80th birthday, and
published in Italy by the Pontifical Academy of Sciences; I have
not seen it. [This article appears in English in the revised,
second edition of the Merton bibliography; see B28, C106.]

It was not deemed bibliographically significant to list and

describe in detail the poetry work-sheets of published poems
and other manuscripts which are housed in the libraries of the
University of Buffalo, the University of Kentucky, Boston
College, and Saint Bonaventure University (which has much
unpublished material). But the major part of Thomas Merton's
manuscripts, published and unpublished, are in the custody of
Sister M. Therese Lentfoehr, of Saint Mary's Hospital, Wausau,
Wisconsin.

I would like to extend to Mr. Richard Bourette, wherever he
may be, my heart-felt thanks for first bringing the writings of
Thomas Merton to my attention; to M. James Fox, O.C.S.O.,
Abbot of Our Lady of Gethsemani, for permission to visit and
work in the Monastery Library; to Thomas Merton for his
invaluable suggestions and assistance and his infinite patience
in answering my numerous queries and occasionally sending me
a flow of items of which I would never have known; to Fr.
Irenaeus Herscher, O.F.M., Librarian of Saint Bonaventure
University, for graciously loaning me the rare, bound volume
of *The Oakhamian* and dispatching from his library the bulk of
Merton's foreign items; to Mr. Robert Giroux, editor-in-chief
of Harcourt, Brace from 1948 to 1955 and now editor and vice
president of Farrar, Straus, and Cudahy, whose counsel and
encouragement made this bibliography possible; to Misses
Naomi Burton and Jean Rosenthal, of Curtis Brown, Ltd., for
their continued interest and help; and to Mr. Christy Dukas
who helped immeasurably in the mechanics of the work.

Special thanks are due to the staffs of the following university
libraries: Columbia, Fordham, and Saint John's (downtown
and uptown branches in Brooklyn), for their response to my
constant research demands; to the members of The New York
Public Library, Reference Department, Room 315, for their
patient help and guidance; to their Newspaper Annex for
rendering invaluable aid and assistance; to Mr. James A.

Wechsler, editor of the New York Post, for permission to work in the newspaper's library.

To the staff of the Central Branch of the Brooklyn Public Library, at Grand Army Plaza, I offer my deep acknowledgement for their efficient help and courteous service and cooperation at all times. Particular thanks are due to Mr. Marino J. Ruffier, Assistant Coordinator of Central Service, for his generous aid in calling errors and omissions to my attention and his kindness in proof-reading the final draft; and to Mr. Theodore Avery, Jr., for his patient help, advice and guidance.

For bringing to my attention omitted items, supplying foreign material and for other bibliographical help, I am thankful also to the late Abbe Robert Kothen, Father P. Leon Van Dijk, O.C.S.O., Annemarie Von Puttkamer, Baroness Elisabeth von Schmidt-Pauli, Mrs. Daniel Gaudin, Mme. Marie Tadie, Mr. Mariano Del Pozo, Father Agostino Gemelli, O.F.M., Father D. Constanzo Somigli, O.S.B., Mr. David Gibble, Sister M. Therese Lentfoehr, S.D.S., Messers. John Brunini and Edward S. Skillin; and to Hollis and Carter, Ltd. of London.

And a final word of thanks and acknowledgement to my [late] wife Mildred, for her diligent application in the laborious task of reading and correcting each draft; her interest in the work had never flagged.

F. D.

Addenda

The following four items, a magazine article and three books, have come to my attention at the completion of the Thomas Merton bibliography which makes it physically impossible to enter them in their respective sections; the entries are:

A hitherto unpublished set of two conferences by Thomas Merton on the priestly life, "Il Sacerdote In Unione Con Maria Immacolata," which has been published in *Convivium*, a new Italian periodical brought out in Rome, Italy, by the Priests' Society for the Adoration of the Blessed Sacrament (1956— Anno I) 26-36. (I have not seen the item.)

Come to the Mountain, text by Thomas Merton. Snowmass, Colorado: Saint Benedict's Cistercian Monastery, 1964.

Christ in the Desert, by Thomas Merton. Abiquiu, New Mexico: Monastery of Christ in the Desert, 1968.

Four Freedom Songs. Commissioned by Robert L. Williams. Words by Thomas Merton. Music by C. Alexander Peloquin. Chicago: G. I. A. Publications, 1968.

Les Voies De La Vraie Priere. Paris: Eds du Cerf, 1973. A translation, by Ceslas Siegfried & Georg Tummer, of *The Climate of Monastic Prayer*.

Zen, Tao Et Nirvana; esprit et contemplation en Extreme-Orient. Paris: Fayard, 1973. A translation by Francis Ledoux, of *Zen and the Birds of Appetite* & *The Way of Chuang Tzu*.

Louis Thomas Merton

1915-1968

Father Louis M. Merton, O.C.S.O., was born on January 31, 1915 in Prades, a French town that nestles below the Pyrenees near Spain, and he died of heart failure on December 10, 1968 in Bangkok, Thailand. He had made the Asian trip to take an active part in a congress of Abbots who were to discuss and consider the renewal of the monastic life in that area of the world.

A. Books and Pamphlets by Thomas Merton

Arranged chronologically

A1 *Thirty Poems* (1944)
First edition:
THIRTY / POEMS / THOMAS MERTON / NEW
DIRECTIONS / THE POETS OF THE YEAR /
NORFOLK: CONNECTICUT
[30] pp., 1 blank leaf. 22 x 16 cm. $1.00. Tan paper
boards lettered in maroon on front cover. Tan dust-wrapper
printed in maroon on front cover.
    Also in paper edition. [30] pp., 1 blank leaf. 22½ x 15
cm. $0.50. Tan dust-wrapper printed in maroon on front
cover. Similar format as bound issue.
    Colophon (p. [29]): Designed for New Directions by
Algot Ringstrom / and printed at The Marchbanks Press,
New York City, in July, 1944 / The Types used are
Kenntonian and Lombardic initials
    [Published: November 20, 1944.]
    The dedication on verso of page [1] which reads: "Virgini
Mariae, Reginae Poetarum / Sanctissimae Dei Genitrici Ac
Semper" should read: "Reginae Poetarum, Sanctissimae Dei
Genitrici / Ac Semper Virgini Mariae"; without Merton's
knowledge the last two words were moved to the beginning of
the dedication.

1

A2 *A Man in the Divided Sea* (1946)
First edition:

A / MAN / IN / THE / DIVIDED / SEA / by /
THOMAS / MERTON
  Title-page enclosed in design consisting of three closely
spaced rectangles forming a border. On verso of title-page:
COPYRIGHT 1946 BY NEW DIRECTIONS / NEW
DIRECTIONS, 500 FIFTH AVE., New York City 18
155 pp., 1 leaf, 1 blank leaf. 23½ x 15½ cm. $2.50.
Black cloth lettered downward in gold on spine.
Oyster-white dust-wrapper, black border, printed in black
and white on front cover and downward on spine in white.
  Colophon (p. [157]): A / MAN IN / THE DIVIDED
SEA / WAS PRINTED AT THE / PRESS OF DUDLEY
KIMBALL. / The type-face used throughout / is
Electra. ROBERT LOWRY / designed the jacket / and
the title / page / V
  [Published: August 25, 1946.]

Contents: Author's Note—Song—Poem: 1939—The Man in
the Wind—Ariadne—The Oracle—Tropics—Fugitive—Ash
Wednesday—Song—Some Bloody Mutiny—Crusoe—Dirge—A
Song—April—The Greek Women—Calypso's Island—The
Pride of the Dead—The Bombarded City—The Storm at Night—
The Ohio River: Louisville—The Dreaming Trader—The House
of Caiphas—Aubade: Harlem—Aubade: The Annunciation—
Dirge for a Town in France—Aubade: The City—The Peril—
Advent—Carol—How Long we Wait—A Letter to my
Friends—The Candlemas Procession—Cana—The Widow of
Nain—St. Paul—Trappists, Working—The Snare—An
Invocation to St. Lucy—St. Thomas Aquinas—St. Alberic—The
Image of True Lovers' Death—The Fall of Night—The
Biography—The Betrayal—Rahab's House—After the Night
Office: Gethsemani—Song for the Blessed Sacrament—The Word:
A Responsory—The Dark Encounter—The Victory—The
Trappist Cemetery: Gethsemani—A Whitsun Canticle (Envoi)—
Ode to the Present Century—St. John Baptist—Clairvaux—La
Salette

This volume also contains all the poems which were published in Thomas Merton's first book of poetry: Thirty Poems; the contents follow (pp. 113-55):

Lent in a Year of War—The Flight into Egypt—Prophet—The Dark Morning—Song for Our Lady of Cobre—The Night Train—Saint Jason—The Messenger—The Regret—Aubade: Lake Erie—Poem—For my Brother—Death—Iphigenia: Politics—The Winter's Night—The Communion—Holy Communion: The City—The Vine—The Evening of the Visitation—In Memory of the Spanish Poet—The Trappist Abbey: Matins—Evening—The Blessed Virgin Mary Compared to a Window—Dirge for the Proud World—The Holy Sacrament of the Altar—Ariadne at the Labyrinth—An Argument: Of the Passion of Christ—St. Agnes: A Responsory—The Holy Child's Song—The Sponge Full of Vinegar

A3 *Guide to Cistercian Life* [1948]
First edition:
Guide / to / Cistercian life / [by Thomas Merton] / [Latin cross imprint] / Our Lady of Gethsemani / Trappist P.O., Kentucky
15 pp. 13½ x 8½ cm. (No Price.) Light blue paper printed in black (n.p., n.d.).

A4 *Cistercian Contemplatives* (1948)
First edition:
CISTERCIAN CONTEMPLATIVES / Monks of the Strict Observance at / OUR LADY OF GETHSEMANI, KENTUCKY / OUR LADY OF THE HOLY GHOST, GEORGIA / OUR LADY OF THE HOLY TRINITY, UTAH / [by Thomas Merton] / A Guide to Trappist Life
62 pp. 23 x 15½ cm. $1.00. Blue-grey boards lettered in maroon on front cover; blue-grey end-papers. No dust-wrapper. 25 black and white photographs.

Also in paper edition. 62 pp. 24 x 16 cm. $0.75. Blue-grey paper printed in maroon on front cover. Similar format as bound issue.

Colophon (p. [63]): This Guide is published by / The Monks of Our Lady Gethsemani / Trappist, Kentucky / A First Edition of 10,000 copies was printed / January MCMXLVIII / by the / Marbridge Printing Company, Inc. / New York

A5 *Figures for an Apocalypse* (1948)
First edition:
FIGURES / FOR AN / APOCALYPSE / by / THOMAS / MERTON

Title-page enclosed in design consisting of three closely spaced rectangles forming a border. On verso of title-page: COPYRIGHT 1947 BY NEW DIRECTIONS / NEW DIRECTIONS, 500 FIFTH AVENUE, / NEW YORK CITY 18

111 pp. 23½ x 15½ cm. $2.50. Black cloth lettered downward in gold on spine. Cream dust-wrapper, black border, printed in black and white on front cover and downward on spine in white.

Colophon (p. [112]): THIS BOOK WAS PRINTED BY / DUDLEY KIMBALL AT HIS PRESS / IN PARSIPPANY, NEW JERSEY

[Published: March 18, 1948.]

Contents: Figures for an Apocalypse—(Advice to my Friends Robert Lax and Edward Rice, to get away while they still can.)—(Cf. Apoc. xiv, 14.)—Landscape, Prophet and Wild-Dog—In the Ruins of New York—Landscape: Beast—The Heavenly City—Landscape: Wheatfields—Two States of Prayer—A Letter to America—Three Postcards from the Monastery—On the Anniversary of my Baptism—Song: Contemplation—A Mysterious Song in the Spring of the Year—Canticle for the Blessed Virgin (Envoi)—Duns Scotus—Two Desert Fathers: St. James, St.

Paul the Hermit—Spring: Monastery Farm—St. John's Night—
The Song of the Traveller—Evening: Zero Weather—The
Transformation: For the Sacred Heart—Rievaulx: St. Ailred—
Theory of Prayer—Clairvaux Prison—Natural History—A
Christmas Card—Winter Afternoon—Freedom as Experience—
The Sowing of Meanings—Pilgrims' Song—The Landfall—The
Poet, to his Book

This volume also contains an essay: Poetry and the
Contemplative Life (pp. 95-111) which was originally
printed in *The Commonweal* (see C14).

A6 *Exile Ends in Glory* (1948)
  First edition:
  Exile / Ends in Glory / The Life of A Trappistine /
  MOTHER M. BERCHMANS, O.C.S.O. / by / Thomas
  Merton / THE BRUCE PUBLISHING COMPANY /
  MILWAUKEE
  3 leaves, vii-xii, 1 leaf, 1-311 pp. 22 x 15 cm. $3.75.
  Grey cloth lettered in black on spine with design.
  Green dust-drapper printed in white on front cover with
  crayon sketch of convent; printed in white on spine.
  Back cover: About the author . . . / THOMAS MERTON
  Errata: back cover of dust-wrapper: par. 3, line 3:
  "Griswold" is spelled "Griswald"; par. 8, line 3: sentence
  reading: "His a talent for beyond" should read: "His
  [is] a talent [far] beyond"; subsequent editions do not
  have comments.
  6 black and white photographs.
  [Published: June 25, 1948.]
  Contents: The Convent of the Redemption—An Interval in
  Lyons—The Convent at Laval—The Novice—Sentence of Exile—
  The Journey—Another Orphanage——At Work in the House of
  God—The Chicken Coop—New Stability—A Vocation Within
  a Vocation—The Child of Mary—At the Gate—A Canticle of
  Gratitude—Mistress of the Novices—"Via Crucis"—"Via
  Crucis"—(continued)—Calvary—Epilogue

A7 *The Seven Storey Mountain* (1948)

  a *First edition*:

    THOMAS MERTON / The Seven Storey / Mountain / [quotation in two lines] / Harcourt, Brace and Company : : New York

      5 leaves, 3-429 pp., 1 blank leaf. 21 x 14 cm. $3.00. Black cloth lettered in gold on spine. Grey dust-wrapper, red-tan spine, printed in black and red on front cover, black and white on spine. On front cover, lower case, a rectangular framed in red with comments printed in black on a white background; on back cover: 3 photographs of Trappist life.

    The binding of the First Edition of The Seven Storey Mountain has an interesting bibliographical history: according to the publisher, of the 6,000 copies which comprised the First Edition, a limited number were bound in off-white cloth (the publisher was unable to furnish the exact amount) lettered in black on spine, and the majority were bound in black cloth lettered in gold on spine. Both the black and off-white bindings are first editions and all bear the words "first edition" on the copyright page.

    Erratum: on verso of leaf 3, top line, Imprimatur heading: "Ex Parte Ordnis" should read: "Ex Parte Ordinis"; the error has been corrected in subsequent printings.

    On verso of title-page: first edition [Published: October 4, 1948.]

Contents: (Part One)—Prisoner's Base—Our Lady of the Museums—The Harrowing of Hell—The Children in the Market Place—(Part Two)—With a Great Price—The Waters of Contradiction—(Part Three)—Magnetic North—True North—The Sleeping Volcano—The Sweet Savor of Liberty—(Epilogue)—Meditatio Pauperis in Solitudine—Index

b *Reprint edition*:
THOMAS MERTON / The Seven Storey / Mountain /
[quotation in two lines] / Garden City Books · Garden City,
New York
  1 blank leaf, 5 leaves, 3-429 pp., 4 blank leaves.
21½ x 14 cm. $1.98. Black cloth lettered in gold on spine.
Light grey dust-wrapper printed in black and red on
front cover and spine.
  On verso of title-page: Garden City Books Reprint
Edition 1951, / by special arrangement with Harcourt,
Brace and Company
  [Published: February 5, 1951.]
c *Paper-back edition*:
  The Seven Storey / Mountain / by / THOMAS
MERTON / [quotation in two lines] / [publisher's
symbol] / A SIGNET BOOK / Published by THE
NEW AMERICAN LIBRARY
  511 [1] pp. 18 x 11 cm. $0.50. Blue and green paper
printed in black, white, yellow and green on front cover
with pictorial scenes showing the gamut of Man's life,
and downward on spine in black and white; edges stained
yellow.
  On verso of title-page: First Printing, April
[30,] 1952
d *Paper-back edition*:
THOMAS MERTON / The Seven Storey / Mountain /
[quotation in two lines] / [publisher's symbol] / IMAGE
BOOKS / A Division of Doubleday & Company, Inc. /
Garden City, New York
  518 pp., 1 leaf. 18 x 10½ cm. $1.95. Crimson and white
paper printed in yellow and black on front cover and
downward on spine.

On verso of title-page: Image Books edition 1970 /
by special arrangement with Harcourt, Brace & World /
Image Books edition published September 1970

A8 *What is Contemplation* (1948)
   a *First edition*:
   What Is Contemplation / by / Thomas Merton, O.C.R. /
   [ornament] / Printed at / Saint Mary's College /
   Notre Dame / Holy Cross, Indiana / 1948
      25 pp., 1 blank leaf. 21½ x 15 cm. $0.50. Salmon paper
   printed in black on front cover [ornament].
      [Published: December 8, 1948.]

   b *English paper-back edition*:
   [Publisher's symbol top and bottom] / THE
   PATERNOSTER SERIES / No. 7 / What is Contem-
   plation? / by / Thomas Merton, O.C.R. / LONDON /
   Burns Oates & Washbourne Ltd. / Publishers to the
   Holy See
      31 pp. 16½ x 10½ cm. Price: 1s. 6d. Brown and grey
   paper printed in brown on front cover.
      On verso of title-page: Made and Printed in Great
   Britain / First published, 1950

A9 *Seeds of Contemplation* (1949)
   a *First edition*:
   Seeds of Contemplation / by Thomas Merton / A NEW
   DIRECTIONS BOOK [device]
      1 blank leaf, 13-201 pp., 2 blank leaves. 22 x 14½ cm.
   $3.00. Tan burlap cloth with pale green label pasted on
   front cover and spine lettered in darker green, downward
   on spine. Cream dust-wrapper, with design, printed in
   black on front cover and downward on spine.
      Colophon (p. [202]): THIS BOOK WAS PRINTED
   BY PETER BEILENSON, / MOUNT VERNON,

NEW YORK, IN THE WEISS AND / CASLON TYPES, ON A SPECIALLY-MADE PAPER. / FEBRUARY MCMXLIX.

[Published: March 2, 1949.]

Contents: Author's Note—Seeds of Contemplation—Everything That is, is Holy—Things in Their Identity—Pray for Your Own Discovery—We Are One Man—A Body of Broken Bones—Solitude—The Moral Theology of the Devil—Integrity—The Root of War is Fear—Hell as Hatred—Faith—Tradition and Revolution—Through a Glass—Qui Non Est Mecum—Humility Against Despair—Freedom Under Obedience—What is Liberty—Detachment—Mental Prayer—Distractions—The Gift of Understanding—The Night of the Senses—The Wrong Flame—Renunciation—Inward Destitution—Contemplata Tradere—Pure Love

b *Signed edition*:

1 leaf, 1 blank leaf, 13-201 pp., 2 blank leaves. 22 x 14½ cm. $7.50. (Similar publication date, format, binding, dust-wrapper as trade edition.) On recto of leaf 1: Of this edition, one hundred copies / have been signed by the author / [signed] Thomas Merton.

Top edges stained green; in brown slip-case.

c *Revised edition*:

5 leaves, xi-xvi, 1-191 pp. 21½ x 13½ cm. $3.00. Off-white sack cloth with cream label pasted on front cover and spine lettered in green, downward on spine.

On verso of title-page: Seventh Printing / First Revised Edition [Published: December 19, 1949.]

In this revised edition, besides "A Preface to the Revised Edition", Chapter 14 reads: "ELECTA UT SOL" which had originally read: "QUI NON EST MECUM". The latter becomes Chapter 15 and follows the original sequence of chapter headings.

10

d *Paper-back edition*:
THOMAS / MERTON / SEEDS OF / CONTEMPLA-
TION / [Christian symbol] / A DELL BOOK
189 [1] pp., 1 leaf. 16 x 11 cm. $0.25. Blue paper
printed in black, white and yellow on front cover and
downward on spine in white; edges stained blue.
On verso of title-page: Published by the Dell Publishing
Company, Inc. / 261 Fifth Avenue, New York 16,
New York
[Published: September 22, 1953.]
This edition has Christian symbols at end of chapters
which were drawn by Rudolf Koch; the table of contents has
been omitted as well as the frontispiece reproduction
of Our Lady of Fontenay (XIIth century; San Vageot)
which was in all the bound editions.
A note from Thomas Merton indicates that "San Vageot" is
a publisher's misprint for the name of the photographer; it
should read: "Yvonne Sauvageot."

A10 *Gethsemani Magnificat* (1949)
First edition:
GETHSEMANI / MAGNIFICAT / CENTENARY OF /
GETHSEMANI ABBEY / [by Thomas Merton] /
[ornament] / MCMXLIX / TRAPPIST, KENTUCKY,
U.S.A.
[72] pp. 30½ x 23 cm. $2.50. Dull blue, pebbled
boards lettered in gold on front cover. A reproduction of
a scene of monks at prayer and the Blessed Mother
standing before them is pasted on front cover on a gold
background within a double, gold border; deep-rose
end-papers. No dust-wrapper.
200 photographs.
Colophon (p. [71]): Designed, printed and lithographed

in U.S.A. / by the Fetter Printing Company,
Louisville, Ky.
[Published: April 5, 1949.]

A11 *The Waters of Siloe* (1949)
 a *First edition*:
  THE WATERS / OF SILOE / THOMAS MERTON /
  Harcourt, Brace and Company New York
   6 leaves, xi-xxxvii, 1 leaf, 3-377 pp. 21½ x 14½ cm.
  $3.50. Light blue cloth with device imprinted in gold
  on front cover; lettered in gold on spine; photographed
  end-papers by Yvonne Sauvageot. Top edges stained blue.
  Green-blue dust-wrapper, with design, printed in white
  and black on front cover and spine.
   36 photographs.
   On verso of title-page: first edition
   [Published: September 5, 1949.]
   Contents: (Part One)—Prologue—Note on the Function of a
   Contemplative Order—Monasticism; St. Benedict; the Cistercians—
   De Rance and La Trappe—The Dispersal; First Trappists in
   America—Foundations in Kentucky and Illinois—The Trappists
   in Nova Scotia; Petit Clairvaux—The Foundation of Gethsemani
   Abbey—Gethsemani in the Nineteenth Century; Other American
   Foundations—Reunion of the Cistercian Congregations; New
   Growth; Gethsemani under Dom Edmond Obrecht—Eight
   American Foundations—A Contemplative Order in Two World
   Wars—The Rising Tide: New Foundations in Georgia, Utah,
   and New Mexico; the Last Mass at Yang Kia Ping—(Part Two)—
   Cistercian Life in the Twelfth Century—The Cistcerian Character
   and Sanctity—Paradisus Claustralis—Bibliography—Glossary of
   some Monastic Terms—Index
 b *Reprint edition*:
  THE WATERS / OF SILOE / THOMAS MERTON /
  Garden City Books • Garden City, N.Y.
   6 leaves, xi-xxxviii, 1 leaf, 3-377 pp. 21 x 14 cm. $1.98.

Alice-blue cloth with device imprinted in gold on front
cover; lettered in gold on spine; photographed end-papers
by Yvonne Sauvageot. Top edges stained green-blue.
Green-blue dust-wrapper, with design, printed in white
and black on front cover and spine.
36 photographs.
On verso of title-page: Garden City Books Reprint
Edition 1951, / by special arrangement with Harcourt,
Brace & Company
[Published: February 5, 1951.]
A number of disparities exist in "A Note on the
Function of a Contemplative Order" in these two editions
which bear mention. In the First Edition (p. xxxiv),
line 18 reads:
"The best religious Order is the one which performs
most faithfully and exactly its own particular function in
the Church, sanctifying its members and saving souls
in the precise way laid down for it in the designs of God
and by the dispositions of the Holy See. This means
that the best Orders are the ones which are able to cling
most closely to the ideal of their founders and to live
their lives most perfectly according to their own
particular Rules."
The Reprint Edition version (p. xxxiv), line 18 reads:
"The best religious Order is the one that has the highest
end and the most perfect means for arriving at that end.
This, at least, is the abstract standard by which we judge
the difference between Orders. But in the concrete,
the Order which comes closest to keeping its own Rule
perfectly and which, at any given moment, best achieves
the end for which it was instituted, will be, in point of fact,
the best one in the Church at that moment. And therefore
one Order cannot improve itself by suddenly deciding

to adopt the institutions and aims of some other Order which has an entirely different purpose in the Church. Instead of becoming better, such an Order would only decline because it would be trying to do a work for which it was never intended."

In the paragraph which deals with Father Garrigou-Lagrange and Father Joret (p. xxxv), line 5, the First Edition does not have a footnote to clarify a point; the Reprint's footnote for line 11 (p. xxxv) reads:

"We must say that the Apostolic life tends principally to contemplation which fructifies in the apostolate." (Garrigou-Lagrange, "The Three Ages of the Interior Life", St. Louis, 1948, Vol. 2, p. 492.) "The life of union with God marks the summit of the Dominican life, the apostolate finds its source there." (Joret, "The Dominican Life", p. 82.)

Finally, in the First Edition (p. xxxvi), line 5, paragraph ends with: ". . . and has too often proved to have been so." This is followed by a new paragraph (line 6) beginning: "A Trappist monastery," etc.; but in the Reprint version (p. xxxvi), line 14, the sentence which reads: ". . . has too often proved to have been so" is followed with these additional comments (same line):

"An even more obvious danger is the materialism into which monks who are also professionally farmers can sometimes fall when they attach more importance to the business of running their farm than to the contemplative life which is their real end. The necessity to maintain industries in order to support their monasteries has also proved to be a considerable hardship to the Trappists. Teaching school may be a work of the active life, but at least it is a highly spiritual activity compared with the brewing of beer, the manufacture of chocolate, and the large-scale marketing of cheese. It was perhaps excessive materialism which really ruined the Cistercian Order in its golden age. The zeal for manual labor as an adjunct to the contemplative life turned into a zest for land-grabbing and business which utterly ruined the contemplative spirit and introduced avarice, and the confusion of much activity, where there should have been the calm recollection that is born of poverty of spirit." This is then followed by a "new" paragraph (p. xxxvi), line 31, which reads: "A Trappist monastery," etc.

c *Paper-back edition*:
The Waters of Siloe / THOMAS MERTON / [publisher's symbol] / IMAGE BOOKS / A Division of Doubleday & Company, Inc. / Garden City, New York 399 pp. 18 x 10½ cm. $1.25. Bluish-green and black paper, with design, printed in black and white on front cover and downward on spine.
On verso of title-page: Image Books edition published September 1962

A12 *The Tears of the Blind Lions* (1949)
First edition:
THOMAS MERTON / THE TEARS / OF THE / BLIND LIONS / NEW DIRECTIONS
32 pp. 21½ x 14 cm. $1.25. Light blue cloth lettered downward on spine in black. Pale blue dust-wrapper printed in brown on front cover and downward on spine.
Also in paper edition. 32 pp. 21 x 13½ cm. $0.50. Pale blue dust-wrapper printed in brown on front cover; supplied with a cream mailing envelope. Similar format as bound issue.
[Published: November 15, 1949.]

Contents: Song—Hymn for the Feast of Duns Scotus—The
Quickening of St. John the Baptist—The Reader—From the
Legend of St. Clement—On a Day in August—Christopher
Columbus—St. Malachy—The Captives: A Psalm—The City After
Noon—In the Rain and the Sun—Dry Places—Je crois en
l'Amour—To the Immaculate Virgin, on a Winter Night—A
Responsory, 1948—A Psalm—Senescente Mundo

A13 *What are These Wounds?* (1950)
First edition:
WHAT ARE / THESE WOUNDS? / THE LIFE OF A
CISTERCIAN MYSTIC / Saint Lutgarde of Aywieres /
By THOMAS MERTON / THE BRUCE PUBLISH-
ING COMPANY / MILWAUKEE
3 leaves, vii-xiv, 1-191 pp. 21½ x 14½ cm. $2.50.
Grey cloth lettered in black on front cover and spine.
Blue dust-wrapper, with picture of nun and imprint
of stigmatic foot, printed in white, pale blue and grey
on front cover, white and grey on spine.
[Published: February 28, 1950.]
Contents: Preface—Childhood. Student in the Benedictine
Convent. Two Suitors. Her First Mystical Graces—Prioress at St.
Catherine's—Aywieres. The Albigensians. Her First Seven Year
Fast—The Souls in Purgatory. Her Power Over Demons. Her
Power of Healing—Sinners—The Spirituality of St. Lutgarde. Her
Mysticism—St. Lutgarde's School of Mysticism at Aywieres.
Relations With the Order of Preachers—Last Years and Death of
St. Lutgarde—After Her Death. Miracles. Cult—Bibliography

A14 *A Balanced Life of Prayer* (1951)
First edition:
A Balanced / Life of Prayer / [ornament] /
THOMAS MERTON, O.C.S.O.
[1]-22 pp., 1 leaf. 15 x 9 cm. $0.10. Cream paper
printed in brown.

On verso of p. 21, lower case: This pamphlet is
published by / The Cistercian Monks of the Strict
Observance / (Trappists) / Copyright 1951 by the
Abbey of Gethsemani / Trappist, Kentucky
[Published: July 30, 1951.]

A15 *The Ascent to Truth* (1951)
   a *First edition*:
   THE / ASCENT / TO / TRUTH / [device] / Thomas
   Merton / [quotation in five lines] / Harcourt, Brace
   and Company, New York
      3 leaves, vii-x, 1 leaf, [3]-342 pp. 22 x 15 cm. $3.50.
   Black cloth with device imprinted in gold on front cover;
   lettered in gold on spine; photographed end-papers by
   Yvonne Sauvageot. Top edges stained red. Shaded blue
   dust-wrapper, with design in grey and red, printed in blue,
   red and white on front cover, blue and white on spine
   with similar design.
      On verso of title-page: first edition
      [Published: September 20, 1951.]
      Contents: Author's Note—Prologue: Mysticism in Man's Life—
   (Part One: The Cloud and the Fire)—Vision and Illusion—The
   Problem of Unbelief—On a Dark Night—False Mysticism—
   Knowledge and Unknowing in Saint John of the Cross—Concepts
   and Contemplation—The Crisis of Dark Knowledge—(Part
   Two: Reason and Mysticism in Saint John of the Cross)—The
   Theological Background—Saint John of the Cross at Salamanca
   and Alcala—The Battle over the Scriptures—Faith and Reason—
   Reason in the Life of Contemplation—"Your Reasonable
   Service"—Between Instinct and Inspiration—Reason and
   Reasoning—Intelligence in the Prayer of Quiet—(Part Three:
   Doctrine and Experience)—The Mirror of Silvered Waters—A
   Dark Cloud Enlightening the Night—The Loving Knowledge of
   God—To the Mountain and the Hill—The Giant Moves in His
   Sleep—(Biographical Notes)—Saint Gregory of Nyssa—Saint
   Bernard of Clairvaux—Saint Thomas of Aquinas— Blessed John

Ruysbroeck—Saint Teresa of Avila—Saint John of the Cross—
Blaise Pascal—John of Saint Thomas—(Sources)

b *Paper-back edition*:
THE / ASCENT / TO / TRUTH / [device] /
Thomas Merton / [quotation in five lines] /
The Viking Press, New York
3 leaves, vii-x, 1 leaf, [3]-342 pp. 19½ x 13 cm. $1.45.
Shaded blue paper, with design in grey and orange,
printed in white on front cover and downward on spine.
On verso of title-page: COMPASS BOOKS EDITION /
ISSUED IN 1959 BY THE VIKING PRESS, INC. /
625 MADISON AVENUE, NEW YORK 22, N.Y.
[Published: August 21, 1959.]

A16 *Devotions to St. John of the Cross* [1953]
First edition:
[A Leaflet] DEVOTIONS / in honor of / SAINT JOHN /
OF THE CROSS / Feastday—November 24th /
[reproduction of St. John of the Cross in supplication] /
Compiled by a cloistered Religious / [Thomas Merton]
8 pp. 13 x 7½ cm. (No price; n.p., n.d.)

A17 *The Sign of Jonas* (1953)
a *First edition*:
THOMAS MERTON / THE SIGN OF JONAS /
HARCOURT, BRACE AND COMPANY /
NEW YORK / [ornament]
1 blank leaf, 6 leaves, 3-362 pp., 1 blank leaf.
22 x 14½ cm. $3.50. Brown cloth with device imprinted
in gold on front cover; lettered in gold on spine;
photographed end-papers. Top edges stained yellow.
Brown dust-wrapper printed in green, white and black on
front cover, green and white on spine.
On verso of title-page: first edition

[Published: February 5, 1953.]

Contents: Prologue—Journey to Nineveh—Solemn Profession—Death of an Abbot—Major Orders—To the Altar of God—The Whale and the Ivy—The Sign of Jonas—Fire Watch, July 4, 1952

b *Paper-back edition*:

[Device] / THE SIGN OF JONAS / [device] / by Thomas Merton / [publisher's symbol] / IMAGE BOOKS / A division of Doubleday & Company, Inc. / Garden City, New York

352 pp., 4 leaves. 18 x 10½ cm. $0.95. Brown paper printed in green, white and black on front cover, green and white on spine.

On verso of title-page: Image Books edition published February, 1956 / 1st printing _____ December, 1955

A18 *Bread in the Wilderness* (1953)

a *First edition*:

[Title-page adorned with photograph of the Head of Le Devot Christ upon which is superimposed the title] BREAD IN THE WILDERNESS [lettered in black reading downward. On verso of leaf 2, lower case, right corner: symbol of Greek cross composed of the name] Thomas Merton [lettered in black forming the horizontal arm, and the words] A NEW DIRECTIONS BOOK [lettered in red reading downward forming the vertical arm]

5 leaves, 1-146 pp., 2 blank leaves. 25½ x 21 cm. $6.00. Red cloth with thin-lined indentation of Latin cross extending the width and length of front cover; lettered downward on spine in black. White dust-wrapper is a reproduction of title-page, with addition of author's name printed in black, lower case, and downward on spine in black.

Errata: p. 24, running head (BREAD IN THE
WILDERNESS) inverted; p. 30, line 25: "imagination
which is no longer able to cope with immaterial" is
repeated on line 27; p. 30, line 26: "and which is incapable
of the simplest efforts to link two terms of" is repeated
on line 28; dust-wrapper, inside back flap, line 20:
"analogy" is spelled "anaology"; these errors, with the
exception of the misspelled word, have been corrected
in the second edition.

Illustrated with photographs of medieval Crucifix
at Perpignan, France, which were taken by J. Comet.

[Published: December 23, 1953.]

Contents: Le Devot Christ—Prologue—(Part I: Psalms and
Contemplation)—Contemplation in the Liturgy—The Testimony
of Tradition—Meanings in Scripture—Songs of the City of God—
Errors to Avoid—(Part II: Poetry, Symbolism and Typology)—
Poetry, Symbolism and Typology—(Part III: Sacraments Scrip-
turarum)—Words as Signs and "Sacraments"—Transformation
in Discovery—"Visible Mysteries"—"When Israel came out of
Egypt"—(Part IV: The Perfect Law of Liberty)—"Thou hast
opened my ears"—From Praise to Ecstasy—(Part V: The Shadow
of Thy Wings)—Dark Lighting—The Silence of the Psalms—
Epilogue—Notes

b *Small, trade edition*:

Identical to First Edition; except red cloth does not
have thin-lined indentation of Latin cross.

5 leaves, 1-146 pp., 2 blank leaves. 23¼ x 17½ cm. $3.50.

[Published: October 31, 1960.]

c *Paper-back edition*:

Same as Small, Trade Edition. From a bibliographical
point of view, it should be noted that the photograph
of the Head of Le Devot Christ in the First Edition
is reproduced in red on the title-page and dust-wrapper.
But in the Small, Trade Edition, the photograph on

the title-page is rendered in grey and red on the dust-wrapper; the paper-back edition, title-page and front cover, is reproduced in grey.

5 leaves, 1-146 pp., 2 leaves. 20½ x 17 cm. $1.65. Cream white paper printed in black on front cover and spine.

[Published: October 31, 1960.]

d *Paper-back edition*:
BREAD IN THE WILDERNESS / Thomas Merton / THE LITURGICAL PRESS / Collegeville / Minnesota
5 leaves, 3-127 pp. 21½ x 14 cm. $1.85. Beige and white paper printed in brown on front cover and downward on spine.

Significantly, this volume does not contain the article on Le Devot Christ, nor the photographs of a medieval Crucifix at Perpignan, France.

[Published: September 15, 1971.]

A19 *The Last of the Fathers* (1954)
First edition:
THOMAS MERTON / The Last of / the Fathers / SAINT BERNARD OF CLAIRVAUX AND THE / ENCYCLICAL LETTER, DOCTOR MELLIFLUUS / [device] / Harcourt, Brace and Company / NEW YORK
123 pp., 2 blank leaves. 23½ x 14½ cm. $3.50.
Green and black cloth with device imprinted in silver on front cover; lettered downward in silver on spine with design; yellow end-papers. Top edges stained yellow. Yellow dust-wrapper, with sketch of XIIth century monastery, printed in brown and blue on front cover and downward on spine.

On verso of title-page: first edition
[Published: June 3, 1954.]

Contents: Preface—Letter from the Cardinal Protector—Letter
from the Abbot General—The Man and the Saint—Saint
Bernard's Writings—Notes on the Encyclical—Encyclical Letter:
Doctor Mellifluus—Bibliography—Index

A20 *No Man is an Island* (1955)
  a *First edition*:
No Man / Is an Island / BY THOMAS MERTON /
[design] / Harcourt, Brace and Company / New York
    4 leaves, ix-xxiii, 1 leaf, 3-264 pp. 21½ x 13½ cm.
\$3.95. Dull royal blue cloth with device imprinted on front
cover; lettered in silver on spine; grey-blue end-papers.
Top edges stained grey-blue. Light grey-blue dust-wrapper,
with design in beige coloring, printed in black and
white on front cover and spine.
    On verso of title-page: first edition
    [Published: March 24, 1955.]
Contents: Author's Note—Prologue—No Man Is An Island—
Love Can Be Kept Only by Being Given Away—Sentences on
Hope—Conscience, Freedom, and Prayer—Pure Intention—The
Word of the Cross—Asceticism and Sacrifice—Being and Doing—
Vocation—The Measure of Charity—Sincerity—Mercy—
Recollection—"My Soul Remembered God"—The Wind Blows
Where It Pleases—The Inward Solitude—Silence
  b *Paper-back edition*:
No Man / Is An Island / BY THOMAS MERTON /
[design] /A DELL BOOK
    254 pp., 1 leaf. 16½ x 10½ cm. \$0.35. Light grey-blue
paper, with design in yellow coloring, printed in black and
white on front cover and downward on spine.
Edges stained yellow.
    On verso of title-page: First Dell printing—
January, 1957
  c *Paper-back edition*:
No Man / Is An Island / by Thomas Merton / [publisher's

22

symbol] / IMAGE BOOKS / A DIVISION OF
DOUBLEDAY & COMPANY, INC. / GARDEN CITY,
NEW YORK
197 pp., 2 leaves. 18 x 10½ cm. $0.95. Light grey-blue
paper, with design in beige coloring, printed in black
on front cover and downward on spine in black and white.
On verso of title-page: Image Books Edition
published September 1967

A21 *The Living Bread* (1956)
  a *First edition*:
  THE / LIVING / BREAD / BY THOMAS MERTON /
  [quotation in three lines] / Farrar, Straus & Cudahy •
  New York [With an Introduction by Gregory Peter XV
  Cardinal Agagianian, Patriarch of Cilicia and of
  Armenia.]
    3 leaves, v-xxxi, 1 leaf, 3-157 pp. 21 x 13½ cm. $3.00.
  Marine blue cloth with device imprinted in gold on
  front cover; lettered in gold on spine. Top edges stained
  grey. Marine blue, mustard shade dust-wrapper, with
  variations of grey and mosaic designs of a symbolic figure
  and chalice, printed in white on front cover and black
  and white on spine.
    On verso of title-page: First printing, 1956
    [Published: March 1, 1956.]
    Contents: Introductory Note—Prologue—[Part] (I [:]
  UNTO THE END)—Christ's Love for Us—Our Response—
  [Part] (II [:] DO THIS IN MEMORY OF ME)—The Christian
  Sacrifice—Worship—Atonement—Agape—[Part] (III [:]
  BEHOLD I AM WITH YOU)—The Real Presence—Sacramental
  Contemplation—The Soul of Christ in the Eucharist—[Part]
  IV [:] I AM THE WAY)—Our Journey to God—The Bread of
  God-Communion and Its Effects—[Part] (V [:] O SACREM
  CONVIVIUM)—Come to the Marriage Feast!—The Eucharist and

the Church—"I Have Called You My Friends"—The New
Commandment—Toward the Parousia
　　The misprint *'Sacrem'* in *'O Sacrem Convivium'* is corrected in
the second printing (*Sacrum*).

　b *Paper-back edition*:
　THOMAS / MERTON / The Living Bread / [quotation
　in three lines] / A DELL BOOK
　　159 pp. 16½ x 10½ cm. $0.35. A variation of blue
　and pale blue paper, with symbolic design, printed in
　purple and black on front cover and downward on spine.
　Edges stained green.
　　On verso of title-page: First Dell printing—
　January, 1959

A22 *Praying the Psalms* (1956)
　a *First paper-back edition*:
　PRAYING THE PSALMS / by / Thomas Merton /
　Drawings by / Grailville Art Center / THE LITURGICAL
　PRESS / Collegeville, Minnesota
　　32 pp. 18 x 12 cm. $0.35. Dark green paper, with
　Christian symbols on front and back cover, printed in
　white on front cover.
　　[Published in 1956.]

　b *English paper-back edition*:
　[Publisher's symbol top and bottom] / THE
　PATERNOSTER SERIES / No. 15 / THE PSALMS
　ARE / OUR PRAYER / by / THOMAS MERTON /
　LONDON / Burns Oates and Washbourne Ltd. /
　Publishers to the Holy See / 1957
　　42 pp., 1 leaf. 16 x 10½ cm. Price: 2s. Light brown
　and beige paper printed in brown on front cover.
　　[Published in 1957.]

A23 *Basic Principles of Monastic Spirituality* (1957)
   a *First paper-back edition*:
      Basic / Principles / of / Monastic / Spirituality / by
      THOMAS MERTON / Abbey of / Gethsemani, /
      Kentucky, / 1957
         35 pp. 23 x 15½ cm. (No Price.) Faded light green
      paper printed in brown on front cover.
      [Published in 1957.]
         Contents: Foreword—I—Quem quaeritis?—II—Verbum caro
      factum est—III—Verbum Crucis—IV—Children of the
      Resurrection—V—Filii et haeredes Dei—VI—Sponsa Christi—
      Epilogue: The monk in a changing world
   b *English paper-back edition*:
      Basic Principles / of / Monastic Spirituality / by /
      Thomas Merton / LONDON / BURNS & OATES
         71 pp. 16 x 10½ cm. Price: 2s. Brownish-crimson paper
      printed in maroon on front cover.
      [Published in 1957.]

A24 *The Silent Life* (1957)
   a *First edition*:
      THE / SILENT / LIFE / BY THOMAS MERTON /
      Farrar, Straus & Cudahy · New York
         2 leaves, v-xiv, 1-178 pp. 21 x 13 cm. $3.50. Brown
      cloth with device imprinted in gold on front cover;
      lettered in gold on spine; photographed end-papers.
      Top edges stained brown. Brown and grey dust-wrapper
      printed in cream white and black on spine. On front cover,
      lower case, a rectangular with title and author's name
      printed in black on a white background. Jacket photo,
      showing the cloister of the Cistercian Abbey of Hauterive,
      Fribourg, Switzerland, is by Benedikt Rast.
         On verso of title-page: First Printing, 1957
      [Published: January 3, 1957.]

Contents: Prologue: What is a Monk?—I THE MONASTIC PEACE—1. Puritas Cordis [Purity of Heart]—2. In Veritate [In Truth]—3. In Laboribus Multis [In Many Labors]—4. In Tabernaculo Altissimi [In the Highest Tabernacle]—5. In Unitate [In Unity]—II THE CENOBITIC LIFE—1. St. Benedict—2. The Benedictines—Solesmes—La Pierre Qui Vire [Primitive Benedictines]—3. The Cistercians—III THE HERMIT LIFE—1. The Carthusians—2. The Camaldolese . . . Index

b *Paper-back edition*:
THE SILENT LIFE / BY THOMAS MERTON / [Christian symbol] / A DELL BOOK
159 pp. 16½ x 11 cm. $0.35. Pink, brown and black paper, with Christian symbols and monks at mass, printed in black, white and blue on front cover and blue and black on spine; edges stained green.

On verso of title-page: First Dell printing— October, 1959

A25 *The Strange Islands* (1957)
First edition:
THE / STRANGE / ISLANDS / POEMS BY THOMAS MERTON / [publisher's name] A NEW DIRECTIONS BOOK [reads upward]
1 blank leaf, 5 leaves, 17-102 pp., 1 blank leaf. 21 x 14 cm. $3.00. Black cloth lettered downward in lavender on spine. Cream-white dust-wrapper printed in black and lavender on front cover and downward on spine.
[Published: March 27, 1957.]

Contents: [Preface]—PART I—How to Enter a Big City—The Guns of Fort Knox—Nocturne—Spring Storm—Whether There Is Enjoyment in Bitterness—Sports Without Blood: A Letter to Dylan Thomas—Exploits of a Machine Age—The Anatomy of Melancholy—Elias: Variations on a Theme—PART II—The Tower of Babel: A Morality—PART III—Birdcage Walk— Landscape—Wisdom—"When in the soul of the serene disciple . . ."—In Silence—Early Mass—A Prelude: For the Feast of St. Agnes—The Annunciation—Sincerity—To a Severe Nun—Elegy for the Monastery Barn—Stranger

A26 *The Tower of Babel* (1957)
Signed edition:
THE / TOWER / OF / BABEL / BY / THOMAS / MERTON [A morality play in two acts which was first published in *Jubilee* magazine (see C96) and reprinted in *The Strange Islands* (see A25). It was also shown on NBC network television, January 27, 1957; condensed and adapted by Richard J. Walsh.]
2 blank leaves, 2 leaves, [7-8]-9-[31] pp., 2 blank leaves. 38½ x 27 cm. $30.00. Bluish-green cloth, tooled ivory cloth spine lettered upward in gold; in grey slip-case.
Colophon (p. [34]): Two hundred and fifty copies of this edition, The Tower of Babel, by Thomas Merton with / woodcuts by Gerhard Marcks, have been printed for James Laughlin in the summer of 1957 / on the hand press by Richard von Sichowsky, Hamburg. The type used is Garamont-Antiqua / from the Lettergeiterij foundry, Amsterdam; the paper was handmade by J. W. Zanders, Duren / and the binding is done by Theophil Zwang, Hamburg. This copy is number 13 / [Signed by the author, Thomas Merton, and the artist, G. Marcks.]
[Published: Summer, 1957.]

A27 *Monastic Peace* (1958)
First edition:
MONASTIC PEACE / By Thomas Merton / ABBEY OF GETHSEMANI
3 leaves, 3-[58] pp., 1 leaf. 23 x 15 cm. $1.00. Beige paper, with Christian symbols, printed in black on front cover.

Colophon (p. [59]): Five thousand copies of Monastic Peace by Thomas Merton have / been printed for the Abbey of Gethsemani by the North Central Pub- / lishing Company, Saint Paul, Minnesota, April, 1958. The type / is Granjon. Art work and layout are by Frank Kacmarcik. The / photographs are by Shirley Burden. The book is sold at the Abbey / of Gethsemani Gatehouse, Trappist P.O., Kentucky, for one dollar.
[Published: April, 1958.]

A28 *Thoughts in Solitude* (1958)
  a *First edition*:
THOMAS / MERTON / THOUGHTS / IN / SOLITUDE / [device] / NEW YORK / FARRAR, STRAUS & CUDAHY
    1 blank leaf, 124 pp., 1 blank leaf. 21 x 13½ cm. $3.00. Orange cloth with device imprinted in gold on front cover; lettered in gold on spine; grey end-papers; top edges stained black. Dark blue and black dust-wrapper, with design, printed in white on front cover, yellow and black on spine.
    On verso of title-page: First Printing, 1958
    [Published: April 8, 1958.]
    Contents: Author's Note—Preface—PART ONE—Aspects of the Spiritual Life—PART TWO—The Love of Solitude

  b *Paper-back edition*:
THOMAS MERTON / THOUGHTS IN / SOLITUDE / [Christian symbol]
    160 pp. 16½ x 11 cm. $0.50. Dark grey paper, with Christian symbol, printed in white and gold on front cover and downward on spine; edges stained green.
    On verso of title-page: First Dell printing— May, 1961

c *Paper-back edition*:
THOMAS MERTON / Thoughts / in / Solitude /
[publisher's symbol] / IMAGE BOOKS / A Division of
Doubleday & Company, Inc. / Garden City, New York
120 pp. 18 x 10½ cm. $0.85. Shaded blue and grey
paper, with Christian symbols, printed in white and
black on front cover and downward on spine in white.
On verso of title-page: Image Books edition
published 1968

A29 *Prometheus / A Meditation* (1958)
PROMETHEUS / A MEDITATION / THOMAS
MERTON / pro manuscripto mcmlviii
[16] pp. 25 x 16 cm. (No Price.) Brown cloth with
white label pasted on spine, lettered upward in brown.
On recto of leaf [5]: Prometheus / A Meditation—
Thomas Merton / Copyright 1958 by the Abbey
of Gethsemani.
Colophon (p. [14]): Privately printed at the Margaret I.
King / Library Press, University of Kentucky, /
Lexington, Spring, 1958. (150 copies) h.c.g. [I have
been unable to track down the signature of the colophon.]

A30 *Nativity Kerygma* (1958)
[Title-page adorned with Christian symbols and the words]
LOGOS [and] NOBIS [read downward side by side
enclosed in a rectangular that resembles an open
prayer book on an altar] / NATIVITY KERYGMA /
BY THOMAS MERTON
[16] pp. 41 x 15½ cm. (No Price.) Beige and dark
tan cloth with allegorical symbols on front and back
cover. Multi-colored end-papers which embrace shades
of purple, lavender, yellow and white.
On verso of title-page: Copyright 1958 by the
Abbey of Gethsemani, Inc.

Colophon (p. [16]) : Nativity Kerygma was written by Thomas Merton / (Father Louis, O.C.S.O.) of the Abbey of Our Lady / of Gethsemani, Trappist, Kentucky. The type is / Times Roman, designed by Stanley Morison. Art work / and layout are by Frank Kacmarcik. The book was composed, / printed by letterpress on Mohawk white Vellum, / and bound by the North Central Publishing Company, / of Saint Paul, Minnesota, the work being completed / on the sixth of December, nineteen-hundred and fifty-eight,
[Published: December 6, 1958.]

A31 *The Secular Journal of Thomas Merton* (1959)
a *First edition*:
The Secular Journal of / THOMAS MERTON / [device] / Farrar, Straus & Cudahy / NEW YORK
4 leaves, vii-xv, 2 leaves, 5-270 pp., 1 blank leaf. 21 x 14 cm. $3.75. Dark grey cloth with TM imprinted in gold on front cover; blue spine lettered across in gold; grey end-papers; top edges stained yellow. Black, yellow and orange dust-wrapper printed in black and white on front cover and downward on spine in black.
[Published: February 2, 1959.]
Contents: Preface—PART 1—Perry Street, New York—PART 2—Cuba—PART 3—New York and St. Bonaventure—PART 4—Interlude: Abbey of Our Lady of Gethsemani—PART 5—St. Bonaventure, Harlem, and Our Lady of the Valley

b *Paper-back edition*:
[Title-page adorned with image of Trappist monk] / The Secular Journal of THOMAS MERTON
223 pp. 16½ x 11 cm. $0.50. Multi-colored paper which embraces purple, lavender, green, brown and orange, printed in white and yellow on front cover and downward on spine in white; edges stained green.

On verso of title-page: First Dell printing—
October, 1960

c *Paper-back edition*:
The Secular Journal of / Thomas Merton / [publisher's
symbol] / IMAGE BOOKS / A Division of Doubleday
& Company, Inc. / Garden City, New York
240 pp. 18 x 10½ cm. $1.25. Blue paper, with design,
printed in orange, white and black on front cover
and downward on spine in white.
On verso of title-page: Image Books edition
published September 1969

A32 *Selected Poems of Thomas Merton* (1959)
a *First American collected edition*:
SELECTED POEMS / of / THOMAS MERTON /
WITH AN INTRODUCTION BY / MARK
VAN DOREN / A NEW DIRECTIONS PAPERBOOK
2 leaves, v-xvii, [1]-139 pp., 1 leaf. 18 x 11 cm. $1.35.
Black and white paper (photograph on cover was taken by
Shirley Burden at Gethsemani Abbey), printed in black
and white on front cover and downward on spine in black.
[Published in 1959.]
Contents: Excerpts from Merton's five books of poetry: 16 from
THIRTY POEMS; 26 from A MAN IN THE DIVIDED SEA;
10 from FIGURES FOR AN APOCALYPSE; 8 from THE
TEARS OF THE BLIND LIONS; 8 from THE STRANGE
ISLANDS; included in this collection are three new poems
appearing for the first time in book form: A Practical Program
for Monks—Song: In the Shows of the Round Ox—An Elegy for
Five Old Ladies; the volume also contains a revised version of
his essay: Poetry and Contemplation: A Reappraisal (it was
originally titled: Poetry and the Contemplative Life (see
paragraph following table of contents in A5; B3; C14))

b *Enlarged edition*:
SELECTED POEMS / of / THOMAS MERTON / WITH
AN INTRODUCTION BY / MARK VAN DOREN /
ENLARGED EDITION / A NEW DIRECTIONS
PAPERBOOK
2 leaves, v-xvii, [1]-140 pp., 1 leaf. 18 x 11 cm. $1.65.
Identical format as preceding edition.
[Published in 1967.]
Contents: Excerpts from Merton's sixth book of verse: 17 from
EMBLEMS OF A SEASON OF FURY (see A41)—This edition
does not contain the essay: Poetry and Contemplation

c *Large format*:
SELECTED POEMS / of / THOMAS MERTON /
WITH AN INTRODUCTION BY / MARK VAN
DOREN / ENLARGED EDITION / A NEW
DIRECTIONS PAPERBOOK
2 leaves, v-xvii, [1]-140 pp., 1 leaf. 20½ x 13½ cm.
$1.75. Identical format as the two preceding editions.
[Published in 1967.]

A33 *Spiritual Direction and Meditation* (1960)
First edition:
[Title] SPIRITUAL DIRECTION / AND
MEDITATION [printed in orange] / BY / THOMAS
MERTON / THE LITURGICAL PRESS
4 leaves, 3-99 pp., 1 blank leaf. 19 x 11½ cm. $2.25.
White cloth, with Christian symbols, lettered in orange on
front cover; orange end-papers. Blue, white and beige
dust-wrapper printed in orange and blue on front cover
and orange on back cover.
[Published in 1960.]

A34 *Disputed Questions* (1960)
a *First edition*:
Thomas Merton / DISPUTED QUESTIONS / Farrar,
Straus and Cudahy : New York

3 leaves, [vi]-xii, 1 leaf, [3]-297 pp., 1 blank leaf.
21 x 14 cm. $3.95. Brown cloth with Thomas Merton
imprinted in brown on front cover; blue cloth spine
lettered downward in silver; top edges stained yellow.
Light brown end-papers. Blue, white, mustard dust-wrapper,
with medieval design, printed in white and brown on
front cover and downward and across on spine in yellow.
On verso of title-page: FIRST PRINTING, 1960
[Published: September 26, 1960.]
Contents: PART ONE—THE PASTERNAK AFFAIR—I.
In memoriam—II. The people with watch-chains—III. Its spiritual
character—MOUNT ATHOS—THE SPIRITUALITY OF
SINAI—St. John of the Ladder—PART TWO—THE POWER
AND MEANING OF LOVE—CHRISTIANITY AND
TOTALITARIANISM—PART THREE—SACRED ART AND
THE SPIRITUAL LIFE—A RENAISSANCE HERMIT:
Blessed Paul Giustiniani—PHILOSOPHY OF SOLITUDE—
LIGHT IN DARKNESS: The Ascetic Doctrine of St. John of the
Cross—THE PRIMITIVE CARMELITE IDEAL—I. The
prophetic spirit—II. Carmelite origins—III. The Fiery Arrow—
IV. Reform and apostolate—V. Carmelite deserts—ABSURDITY
IN SACRED DECORATION—ST. BERNARD: MONK AND
APOSTLE—APPENDIX A—APPENDIX B

b *Paper-back edition*:
DISPUTED / QUESTIONS / Thomas Merton /
[publisher's symbol] / A MENTOR-OMEGA BOOK /
Published by The New American Library
222 pp., 1 leaf. 18 x 11 cm. $0.75. White and orange
paper, with design, printed in black on front cover
and downward on spine in orange and black.
On verso of title-page: First Printing, April, 1965

A35 *The Behavior of Titans* (1961)
First edition:
[Device in red atop title-page] / The Behavior of Titans /
by Thomas Merton / A NEW DIRECTIONS BOOK

1 blank leaf, 6 leaves, 11-106 pp., 3 blank leaves.
25 x 16½ cm. $3.50. Red cloth with device imprinted on
front cover, lettered downward on spine in gold. Cream
colored dust-drapper, with device, printed in red and
black on front cover and downward on spine.
[Published: March 27, 1961.]
    The Contents [:]—PART ONE—The Behavior Of Titans—
1. Prometheus—A Note: Two Faces of Prometheus—Prometheus:
A Meditation—2. Atlas And The Fat Man—PART TWO—The
Guilty Bystander—1. Letter To An Innocent Bystander—2. A
Signed Confession Of Crimes Against The State—PART
THREE— Herakleitos The Obscure—1. Herakleitos: A Study—
2. The Legacy Of Herakleitos
    The chapter "Prometheus: A Meditation" was originally issued
in a privately printed edition (see A29).

A36 *The New Man* (1962)

a *First edition*:

THOMAS MERTON / The New Man / FARRAR,
STRAUS & CUDAHY / NEW YORK
    1 blank leaf, 5 leaves, [3]-248 pp., 1 blank leaf.
21 x 13 cm. $3.50. Orange cloth with TM imprinted in
silver on front cover. Black cloth spine, lettered across
in silver. White dust-wrapper printed in orange and
black on front cover and downward on spine.
    [Published: January 4, 1962.]
    [Contents:] THE WAR WITHIN US—PROMETHEAN
THEOLOGY—IMAGE AND LIKENESS—FREE SPEECH—
[Parrhesia]—SPIRIT IN BONDAGE—THE SECOND
ADAM—LIFE IN CHRIST—SACRAMENTAL ILLUMINA-
TION—CALLED OUT OF DARKNESS

b *Paper-back edition*:

The New Man / [two closely spaced lines] / by
THOMAS MERTON / [publisher's symbol] / A
MENTOR-OMEGA BOOK / Published by The New
American Library

141 pp., 1 leaf. 18 x 11 cm. $0.60. Black and brown
paper, with symbolic design, printed in white on front
cover and downward on spine in red.
On verso of title-page: First Printing, December, 1963

A37 *New Seeds of Contemplation* (1962)
  a *First edition*:
New Seeds of / Contemplation / Thomas Merton /
A NEW DIRECTIONS BOOK
1 blank leaf, 4 leaves, ix-xv, 1 leaf, 1-297 pp., 3 blank
leaves. 21 x 14½ cm. $4.50. Dark green cloth lettered
in silver and gold on spine, with design in gold between
title and author. Cream colored dust-wrapper, with
designs in silver and gold on front and back cover and spine,
printed in black on front cover and spine.
[Published: January 30, 1962.]
(More than twelve years have passed between the first
and second redactions of this text (see table of contents in
A9, b & c); the listing that follows indicates new
chapters.)
Contents: PREFACE—AUTHOR'S NOTE—1. WHAT IS
CONTEMPLATION?—2. WHAT CONTEMPLATION IS
NOT—12. THE PURE HEART—15. SENTENCES—19. FROM
FAITH TO WISDOM—22. LIFE IN CHRIST—33. JOURNEY
THROUGH THE WILDERNESS—39. THE GENERAL
DANCE

(What follows are changes in chapter headings; the
titles in parenthesis refer to the Revised Edition and
those in square brackets to NEW SEEDS.)
Contents: (SOLITUDE)—[11. LEARN TO BE ALONE]—
(THROUGH A GLASS)—[21. THE MYSTERY OF
CHRIST]—(ELECTA UT SOL)—[23. THE WOMAN
CLOTHED WITH THE SUN]—(QUI NON EST MECUM)—
[24. HE WHO IS NOT WITH ME IS AGAINST ME]—

(CONTEMPLATA TRADERE)—[37. SHARING THE FRUITS OF CONTEMPLATION]

(And finally, in the Revised Edition, chapter 4, WE ARE ONE MAN (22-37), becomes in NEW SEEDS three chapters which are: 7. UNION AND DIVISION; 8. SOLITUDE IS NOT SEPARATION; 9. WE ARE ONE MAN.)

b *Paper-back edition*:
New Seeds of / Contemplation / Thomas Merton / A NEW DIRECTIONS BOOK

4 leaves, ix-xv, 1 leaf, 1-297 pp., 1 leaf, 1 blank leaf. 20½ x 13½ cm. $2.25. Light grey paper, with design, printed in black on front cover and downward on spine. [Published in 1972.]

A38 *Original Child Bomb* (1962)
a *First trade edition*:
[Title-page adorned with coal-black drawing by Emil Antonucci of an exploding atom bomb] / ORIGINAL CHILD BOMB / points for meditation to be scratched on the walls of a cave / THOMAS MERTON

[28] pp. 23½ x 22½ cm. $1.95. Black cloth with splashes of orange lettered in white on front and back cover, downward on spine. No dust-wrapper.

On verso of title-page, printed upward: A NEW DIRECTIONS BOOK [Copyright, 1962 by The Abbey of Gethsemani, Inc. Library of Congress Catalog Card Number 61-18524. Cum permissu superiorum.]

Colophon (p. [26]): This book was designed / and illustrated by Emil Antonucci. / The type face is News Gothic Bold. / 8000 copies were printed for New Directions by Century Letter Company in December, 1961. / 500

copies were bound in Fabriano paper and signed by
the author.
[Published: March 21, 1962.]
b *Limited signed edition*:
(Similar publication date, format and binding
as the Trade Edition.)
[28] pp. 23½ x 23 cm. $7.50. Black cloth with white
label pasted on front and back cover lettered in black.
Supplied with plain cellophane wrapper.
Colophon (p. [26]): [. . .] 500 copies were bound
in Fabriano paper and signed by the author. /
[signature] Thomas Merton

A39 *A Thomas Merton Reader* (1962)
First edition:
Edited by THOMAS P. MCDONNELL / [device] /
A Thomas Merton Reader / HARCOURT, BRACE
& WORLD, INC., NEW YORK
1 blank leaf, 3 leaves, vii-xix, 1 leaf, 3-553 pp., 2 blank
leaves. 22 x 15 cm. $5.75. Grey cloth with TM imprinted in
grey on front cover. Light red spine lettered downward
and across in gold. Top edges stained light red. Light
red dust-wrapper, with design, printed in white,
black and gold on front cover and across on spine
in white and gold.
On verso of title-page: FIRST EDITION
[Published: October 24, 1962.]
Contents: First and Last Thoughts: An Author's Preface—
Excerpts from Merton's following books: A1, A2, A5, A7, A11,
A12, A15, A17, A18, A20, A25, A26, A29, A30, A32, A33,
A35, A37, B9; included in this collection are eight articles
appearing for the first time in book form: Letter to Aleksei Surkov;
The Letters of St. Bernard; Religion and the Bomb; Prayer for
Peace; Christian Culture Needs Oriental Wisdom; Conquistador,

Tourist, and Indian; The Good Samaritan; Theology of
Creativity; plus two pieces from *New Directions* 17: Jorge
Carrera Andrade, and The Recovery of Paradise (see B41); The
Wisdom of the Desert, from *The Wisdom of the Desert*, a book
translated by Merton (see D4); two book reviews: Laughter in the
Dark, and The World's Body (see C1 & C2); finally, three
segments of unpublished material from the original ms. of *The
Seven Storey Mountain*: In The Monastic Community; Christmas
Night; The Ways of Love

A40 *Life and Holiness* (1963)

a *First edition*:

THOMAS MERTON / LIFE AND HOLINESS /
HERDER AND HERDER

1 blank leaf, 3 leaves, vii-xii. 2 leaves, 3-162 pp.,
1 blank leaf. 20½ x 13 cm. $3.50. Cream white cloth
with TM imprinted in blue on front cover and lettered
downward on spine. White dust-wrapper printed in blue
and black on front cover and downward on spine.

[Published: Spring, 1963.]

Contents: Introduction—I Christian Ideals—II The Testing of
Ideals—III Christ, the Way—IV The Life of Faith—V Growth
in Christ

b *Paper-back edition*:

THOMAS MERTON / LIFE AND HOLINESS /
[publisher's symbol] / IMAGE BOOKS / A Division
of Doubleday & Company, Inc. / Garden City, New York

119 pp. 18 x 10½ cm. $0.75. Purple paper, with
Christian symbols, printed in white, black and yellow
on front cover, downward on spine in yellow and white.

On verso of title-page: Image Books Edition
published September, 1964

A41 *Emblems of a Season of Fury* (1963)
First edition:

EMBLEMS OF A / SEASON OF FURY / THOMAS
MERTON / A NEW DIRECTIONS PAPERBOOK

2 leaves, v-vi, 1 leaf, 3-149 pp., 2 leaves. 18 x 11 cm. $1.65. Black and grey paper printed in white on front cover and downward on spine. Upper part of cover is adorned with a detail from welded steel sculpture "Manes Flayed ♯2" by Ezio Martinelli. Photo: Oliver Baker, Courtesy The Willard Gallery, New York. [Published: December 20, 1963.]

(The contents that follow list only those poems which mark their first appearance in book form.)

Contents: And So Goodbye to Cities—Gloss on the Sin of Ixion—Macarius and the Pony—Macarius the Younger—Song for the Death of Averroes—A Dream at Arles on the Night of the Mistral—Song: If You Seek . . . —Seven Archaic Images—To Alfonso Cortes—News from the School at Chartres—What to Think When It Rains Blood

(*Emblems* contains two pieces of prose: Hagia Sophia which was issued in an edition of 69 copies (Lexington: Stamperia del Santuccio; 1962; see E16); A Letter to Pablo Antonio Cuadra Concerning Giants appears here in a revised form; it was published in *A Thomas Merton Reader* bearing the title: Conquistador, Tourist, and Indian (see A39).)

(Besides the verse and prose, *Emblems* has a section of translations (by Merton) of the work of other poets: Vallejo (Peru), Carrera Andrade (Ecuador), Cuadra, Cardenal and Cortes (Nicaragua), and mystical poems by Raissa Maritain (wife of the Thomist philosopher). Merton renders short sketches of the poets; the biographical piece, Jorge Carrera Andrade, appeared in the *Merton Reader* (see A39). The selections are from *New Directions* 17 (see B41).)

Two poems by Cortes; "The Flower of the Fruit" and "Space Song," were translated by Thomas Merton and appeared in *The Sewanee Review*, LXXI. 3 (July-September 1963) [466]-467.

A42 *Seeds of Destruction* (1964)

a *First edition*:

Seeds / of / Destruction / [horizontal line across
title-page] / By THOMAS MERTON / NEW YORK
[short vertical line] Farrar, Straus and Giroux
  1 blank leaf, 5 leaves, xi-xvi, 1 leaf, 3-328 pp., 3 blank
leaves. 21 x 13 cm. $4.95. Black cloth, light red spine
lettered across and downward in black. Grey end-papers;
top edges stained light red. White dust-wrapper, with
design in grey, brown and orange, printed in black
on front cover and downward on spine.
  On verso of title-page: First Printing, 1964
[Published: November 16, 1964.]
Contents: Author's Note—PART ONE: BLACK REVOLU-
TION—I. Letters to a White Liberal—II. The Legend of Tucker
Caliban—PART TWO: THE DIASPORA—I. The Christian in
World Crisis—II. The Christian in the Diaspora—III. A Tribute
to Gandhi—PART THREE: LETTERS IN A TIME OF CRISIS

b *Paper-back edition*:

Seeds / of Destruction / [horizontal line across
title-page] / By THOMAS MERTON / The Macmillan
Company [short vertical line] NEW YORK
  224 pp. 18 x 10½ cm. $1.45. Green paper, with device,
printed in white and black on front cover and
downward on spine.
  On verso of title-page: First Macmillan Edition 1967

A43 *The Way of Chuang Tzu* (1965)

a *First edition*:

[Title-page adorned with early Chinese drawing]
THE WAY OF / CHUANG TZU / BY THOMAS
MERTON / NEW DIRECTIONS
  159 pp., 1 blank leaf. 21 x 14½ cm. $4.00. White cloth
with design imprinted in black on front cover, lettered

40

downward on spine in black. White dust-wrapper,
with early Chinese drawing, printed in black and orange
on front cover and downward on spine.
On verso of title-page: First printing
[Published: November 10, 1965.]
  b *Paper-back edition*:
[Title-page adorned with early Chinese drawing]
THE WAY OF / CHUANG TZU / BY THOMAS
MERTON / NEW DIRECTIONS
159 pp. 20½ x 13½ cm. $1.75. White paper, with
early Chinese drawing, printed in black on front cover
and downward on spine.

A44 *Seasons of Celebration* (1965)
First edition:
THOMAS MERTON / SEASONS / OF / CELEBRA-
TION / Farrar, Straus and Giroux / NEW YORK
2 leaves, v-vi, 1 leaf, 1-248 pp. 21 x 13½ cm. $4.95.
Black cloth lettered downward on spine in gold; top edges
stained a dull pink; mustard colored end-papers. Yellow,
green and orange dust-wrapper printed in green and
black on front cover and downward on spine.
On verso of title-page: First Printing, 1965
[Published: December 3, 1965.]
Contents: Author's Note—LITURGY AND SPIRITUAL
PERSONALISM—CHURCH AND BISHOP IN ST IGNATIUS
OF ANTIOCH—TIME AND THE LITURGY—THE
SACRAMENT OF ADVENT IN THE SPIRITUALITY OF ST
BERNARD—ADVENT: HOPE OR DELUSION?—THE
NATIVITY KERYGMA (see A30)—ASH WEDNESDAY—
CHRISTIAN SELF-DENIAL—EASTER: THE NEW LIFE—A
HOMILY ON LIGHT AND THE VIRGIN MARY—THE
GOOD SAMARITAN (see table of contents in A39)—THE
NAME OF THE LORD—"IN SILENTIO" (condensed from

the Introduction: Silence in Heaven; see B27)—COMMUNITY
OF PARDON—LITURGICAL RENEWAL: THE OPEN
APPROACH

A45 *Raids on the Unspeakable* (1966)
First edition:
Raids on the / Unspeakable / Thomas Merton /
NEW DIRECTIONS
5 leaves, 182 pp. 20½ x 13½ cm. $1.95. Grey paper
printed in black on front cover and downward on spine
in white. Cover photograph by Thomas Merton;
design by David Ford.
[Published: August 9, 1966.]
Contents: PROLOGUE—RAIN AND THE RHINOCEROS—
TO EACH HIS DARKNESS—FLANNERY O'CONNOR: A
PROSE ELEGY—A DEVOUT MEDITATION IN MEMORY
OF ADOLF EICHMANN—LETTER TO AN INNOCENT
BYSTANDER—THE TIME OF THE END IS THE TIME OF
NO ROOM—PROMETHEUS: A MEDITATION (see A29)—
ATLAS AND THE FATMAN—MARTIN'S PREDICAMENT,
or ATLAS WATCHES EVERY EVENING—THE EARLY
LEGEND—READINGS FROM IBN ABBAD—MESSAGE TO
POETS—ANSWERS ON ART AND FREEDOM—
SIGNATURE: NOTES ON THE AUTHOR'S DRAWINGS
See table of contents in A35 for "Letter to an Innocent
Bystander" and "Atlas and the Fatman."

A46 *Monastic Life at Gethsemani* (1966)
First edition:
MONASTIC LIFE AT GETHSEMANI / [By
Thomas Merton]
[32] pp. 20½ x 20 cm. (No Price.) White paper,
with photograph and Christian symbol, printed in black
on front cover. Light green end-papers. Back cover
adorned with small photograph, printed in orange:
ABBEY OF GETHSEMANI / TRAPPIST, KY. / 40073

Colophon (p. [32]): Text and Photos MONKS OF
GETHSEMANI / Design Peter Geist / Printing
WESTERN PRINTING AND / LITHOGRAPHING
COMPANY

A47 *Gethsemani / A Life of Praise* (1966)
First edition:
GETHSEMANI / A LIFE OF PRAISE / Text by
Thomas Merton / [Copyright] ABBEY OF
GETHSEMANI 1966
[64] pp. 28½ x 22 cm. (No Price.) White cloth with
a black rectangular superimposed on front cover lettered
in gold within a single, gold border and downward on spine.
Deep brown, photographed end-papers. Grey and brown
dust-wrapper, with photographs of monks on front and
back cover, printed in white on front cover and downward
on spine. Inside flap, back cover: DESIGN: PETER
GEIST / PHOTOGRAPHS BY: ART FILMORE /
BROTHER EPHREM / BROTHER PIUS / PRINTING:
PINAIRE LITHOGRAPHING CORP.
[Published: 1966.]

A48 *Conjectures of a Guilty Bystander* (1966)
a *First edition*:
CONJECTURES OF A / GUILTY BYSTANDER /
by Thomas Merton / [quotation in six lines] /
1966 DOUBLEDAY & COMPANY, INC.
GARDEN CITY, NEW YORK
2 leaves, [v]-vii, 1 leaf, [3]-328 pp. 21½ x 14½ cm.
$4.95. Brown cloth, beige spine lettered across and
downward in black. Mustard colored end-papers.
Deep brown dust-wrapper printed in white, green and
lavender on front cover, across and downward on spine.
On verso of title-page: First Edition
[Published: November 4, 1966.]

b *Paper-back edition*:
THOMAS MERTON / CONJECTURES OF A /
GUILTY BYSTANDER / [quotation in six lines] /
[publisher's symbol] / IMAGE BOOKS / A Division of
Doubleday & Company, Inc. / Garden City, New York
360 pp. 18 x 11 cm. $1.25. Multicolored paper which
embrace shades of yellow, green, grey, blue and black,
with Christian symbols, printed in green, white, orange
and blue on front cover, downward on spine in
orange and black.
On verso of title-page: Image Books edition
published February 1968

A49 *Mystics and Zen Masters* (1967)
a *First edition*:
Thomas / Merton / MYSTICS AND / ZEN MASTERS /
[device] / FARRAR, STRAUS AND GIROUX /
NEW YORK
1 blank leaf, 3 leaves, [vii]-x, 1 leaf, [3]-303 pp.,
1 blank leaf. $21\frac{1}{2}$ x $14\frac{1}{2}$ cm. $5.50. Black cloth with TM
imprinted in gold on front cover. Lettered across on spine
in gold and orange with design. Brown end-papers;
top edges stained orange. White dust-wrapper printed
in black and orange on front cover and across on spine
with design. Back cover: photo of Thomas Merton
by Edward Rice.
On verso of title-page: First printing, 1967
[Published: May 5, 1967.]
Contents: MYSTICS AND ZEN MASTERS—CLASSIC
CHINESE THOUGHT—LOVE AND TAO—THE JESUITS
IN CHINA— FROM PILGRIMAGE TO CRUSADE—
VIRGINITY AND HUMANISM IN THE WESTERN
FATHERS—THE ENGLISH MYSTICS—SELF-KNOWLEDGE
IN GERTRUDE MORE AND AUGUSTINE BAKER—

RUSSIAN MYSTICS—PROTESTANT MONASTICISM—
PLEASANT HILL—CONTEMPLATION AND DIALOGUE—
ZEN BUDDHIST MONASTICISM—THE ZEN KOAN—THE
OTHER SIDE OF DESPAIR—BUDDHISM AND THE
MODERN WORLD—NOTES

b *Paper-back edition*:
MYSTICS / & / ZEN / MASTERS / [horizontal line
across title-page] / Thomas Merton / [publisher's
symbol] / A DELTA BOOK
1 blank leaf, 3 leaves, [vii]-x, 1 leaf, [3]-303 pp.,
2 blank leaves. 20½ x 13½ cm. $1.95. Cream white paper,
with symbols, printed in black on front cover and
downward on spine.
On verso of title-page: First Delta printing—
March 1969

A50 *The Plague* (1968)
First edition:
Religious Dimensions in Literature / Lee A. Belford,
General Editor / ALBERT CAMUS' / The Plague /
Introduction and Commentary by / THOMAS MERTON /
[publisher's symbol] THE SEABURY PRESS ·
NEW YORK
43 pp. 20½ x 14 cm. $0.85. Black and dull red paper
printed in white and black on front and back cover.
[Published in 1968.]

A51 *Cables to the Ace* (1968)
a *First edition*:
CABLES TO THE ACE / or / Familiar Liturgies of /
Misunderstanding / THOMAS MERTON / A NEW
DIRECTIONS BOOK
1 blank leaf, 2 leaves, 1-60 pp., 1 blank leaf. 21 x 14½ cm.
$3.75. Black cloth lettered downward on spine in white.

Black dust-wrapper printed in white on front cover
and downward on spine. Cover: Semiotic poem by
J. Blaine. Design: David Ford.
On verso of title-page: First Edition
[Published: March 31, 1968.]

b *Paper-back edition*:
CABLES TO THE ACE / or / Familiar Liturgies of /
Misunderstanding / THOMAS MERTON / A NEW
DIRECTIONS BOOK
2 leaves, 1-60 pp. 20½ x 13½ cm. $1.25. Black paper,
identical cover and design as dust-wrapper of hard
cover edition; same publication date.

A52 *Faith and Violence* (1968)
First edition:
Faith and / Violence / Christian Teaching and / Christian
Practice / Thomas Merton / UNIVERSITY OF
NOTRE DAME PRESS / 1968
2 leaves, vi-x, 1 leaf, 3-291 pp., 1 blank leaf. 20½ x 13½
cm. $1.95. White paper printed in black and violet on
front cover and downward on spine.
[Published: July 10, 1968.]

Contents: Preface—PART ONE— Toward a Theology of
Resistance—Blessed Are the Meek—Non-Violence and the
Christian Conscience—Peace and Protest—The Prison
Meditations of Father Delp—An Enemy of the State—Pacifism
and Resistance in Simone Weil—PART TWO—Vietnam: an
Overwhelming Atrocity—Is Man a Gorilla with a Gun?—Nhat
Hanh Is My Brother—Taking Sides on Vietnam—A Note on The
Psychological Causes of War by Eric Fromm—PART THREE—
From Non-Violence to Black Power—Religion and Race in the
United States—Events and Pseudo-Events—The Hot Summer of
Sixty-Seven—The Meaning of Malcolm X—PART FOUR—
Violence and the Death of God: or God as Unknown Soldier—
The Unbelief of Believers—Apologies to an Unbeliever—The

Contemplative Life in the Modern World—Honest to God—
The Death of God and the End of History—"Godless
Christianity"?—Index

A53 *Zen and the Birds of Appetite* (1968)
  a *First edition*:
    ZEN / AND THE / BIRDS OF APPETITE /
    THOMAS MERTON / A NEW DIRECTIONS BOOK
      1 blank leaf, 4 leaves, ix-[x-xii], 1-141 pp., 4 blank leaves.
    21 x 14 cm. $5.25. Light blue cloth lettered downward
    on spine in gold. Grey, black, white dust-wrapper printed
    in black on front cover, downward on spine. Cover:
    from the scroll painting "Haboku Landscape" by Sesshu
    (1420-1506) in The Cleveland Museum of Art (Gift of the
    Norweb Foundation). Photograph, by courtesy of
    The Asia Society, New York. Design by David Ford.
    [Published: October 31, 1968.]
      Contents: Author's Note—PART ONE—The Study of Zen—
    New Consciousness—A Christian Looks at Zen—D.T. Suzuki:
    The Man and his Work—Nishida: A Zen philosopher—
    Transcendent Experience—Nirvana—Zen in Japanese Art—
    Appendix: Is Buddhism Life-Denying?—PART TWO—Wisdom
    in Emptiness, A Dialogue: D. T. Suzuki and Thomas Merton—
    Postface
      "Wisdom in Emptiness, A Dialogue: D. T. Suzuki and Thomas
    Merton" was first published in *New Directions* 17 (see B41).

  b *Paper-back edition*:
    ZEN / AND THE / BIRDS OF APPETITE /
    THOMAS MERTON / A NEW DIRECTIONS BOOK
      4 leaves, ix-[x-xii], 1-141 pp., 3 blank leaves. 20½ x 14
    cm. $1.75. Grey, black, white paper, identical photo and
    design as dust-wrapper of hard cover edition;
    same publication date.

A54 *The True Solitude* (1969)
First edition:
The True Solitude / [on the verso of leaf 1 is the subtitle]
SELECTIONS FROM THE WRITINGS OF [and the
author's name follows across to the title-page]
Thomas Merton / SELECTED BY DEAN WALLEY /
[publisher's symbol] / [a horizontal line below symbol] /
HALLMARK EDITIONS
1 blank leaf, 1 leaf, [1]-[62] pp., 1 blank leaf. 19½ x 12
cm. $2.50. Dark blue cloth lettered in light blue on front
cover and downward on spine. Blue dust-wrapper
printed in white on front cover and downward on spine.
Colophon (p. [62]): Composed in linotype Aldus,
with handset Palatino / Swash capitals. Aldus and Palatino
are based on / 16th century Venetian type styles and
were designed / by Hermann Zapf. Typography by /
Grant Dahlstrom, set at the Castle Press. / Printed on
Hallmark Eggshell Book paper. / Designed by
Harald Peter.
[Published: 1969.]
Contents: Introduction—World of Solitude—The Discovery of
God—The Way to Peace—Day of a Stranger
The selections in this book were taken from the following works
of Thomas Merton: A7, A9, A17, A20, A21, A32, A37, A48;
"Day of a Stranger" originally appeared in the *Hudson Review*
(see C318).

A55 *My Argument with the Gestapo* (1969)
First edition:
THOMAS MERTON / My Argument / With The
Gestapo / A MACARONIC JOURNAL / DOUBLEDAY
& COMPANY, INC., GARDEN CITY, NEW
YORK, 1969
259 pp., 3 blank leaves. 21½ x 14½ cm. $4.95.
Maroon and black cloth lettered downward on spine

in silver. Black dust-wrapper printed in white and red
on front cover and downward on spine; back cover:
a youthful photograph of Thomas Merton.
    On verso of title-page: First Edition
    [Published: July 3, 1969.]

A56 *Contemplative Prayer* (1969)
  a *First edition*:
    THOMAS MERTON / CONTEMPLATIVE PRAYER /
    HERDER AND HERDER
        144 pp. 21 x 14 cm. $4.50. Black cloth lettered downward
    on spine in violet. Violet end-papers. Black dust-wrapper,
    with photograph of Thomas Merton on front cover by
    John Howard Griffin, printed in violet and blue on
    front cover and downward on spine.
        [Published: September 6, 1969.]
        This book is being published in Ireland as Number One of the
    Cistercian Studies Series under the title THE CLIMATE OF
    MONASTIC PRAYER [copyright], 1969 by the Thomas Merton
    Legacy Trust.

  b *Paper-back edition*:
    CONTEMPLATIVE / PRAYER / THOMAS MERTON /
    [publisher's symbol] IMAGE BOOKS / A DIVISION
    OF DOUBLEDAY & COMPANY, INC. / GARDEN
    CITY, NEW YORK
        116 pp. 2 leaves. 18 x 10½ cm. $0.95. Dark grey paper,
    with photograph of Thomas Merton on front cover by
    John Howard Griffin, printed in white and yellow
    on front cover and downward on spine.
        On verso of title-page: IMAGE BOOKS EDITION
    PUBLISHED FEBRUARY, 1971

A57 *The Geography of Lograire* (1969)
  a *First edition*:
    THE GEOGRAPHY OF / LOGRAIRE / THOMAS
    MERTON / A NEW DIRECTIONS BOOK

1 blank leaf, 3 leaves, 1-153 pp., 1 blank leaf.
21 x 14 cm. $4.95. Light grey cloth lettered downward on
spine in pink. Black dust-wrapper printed in white on
front cover and downward on spine. Cover photo by
Wynn Bullock; design by David Ford; back cover: photo
of Thomas Merton by John Howard Griffin.
[Published: October 15, 1969.]

Contents: Author's Note—Prologue: The Endless Inscription—
SOUTH—I "Will a narrow lane save Cain?"—II "Roar of
red wood racer eats field."—III Hymns of Lograire—IV Miami
You Are About to Be Surprised—V Two Moralities—1. Thonga
Lament (Africa)—2. Hare's Message (Hottentot)—VI A
Clever Stratagem; or, How to Handle Mystics—VII Notes for a
New Liturgy—VIII Ce Xochitl: The Sign of Flowers (Mexico)—
IX The Ladies of Tlatilco—X Chilam Balam (Yucatan)— XI
Dzules (Yucatan)—NORTH—Prologue: Why I Have a Wet
Footprint on Top of My Mind—I Queens Tunnel—II "There is a
grain of sand in Lambeth which Satan cannot find"—III The
Ranters and Their Pleads (London)—IV Kane Relief Expedition—
EAST—Love of the Sultan—I East with Ibn Battuta—1. Cairo
1326—2. Syria—3. The Nusayris—4. Mecca—5. Isfahan—6.
Delhi—7.Calicut—II East with Malinowski: Tupuseleia—III Cargo
Songs—IV Place Names—V Tibud Maclay—VI Sewende (Seven
Day)—VII Cargo Catechism—VIII John the Volcano—IX Dialog
with Mister Clapcott—X And a Few More Cargo Songs—WEST—
I Day Six O'Hare Telephane—II At This Precise Moment of
History—III Ghost Dance: Prologue—IV Ghost Dance—Source
Notes

b *Paper-back edition*:
THE GEOGRAPHY OF / LOGRAIRE / THOMAS
MERTON / A NEW DIRECTIONS BOOK
    3 leaves, 1-153 pp. 20½ x 13½ cm. $1.75. Black paper,
identical photo and design as dust-wrapper of hard cover
edition; back cover does not have photograph of
Thomas Merton.
    [Published: October 15, 1969.]

A58 *Opening the Bible* (1971)
First edition:
OPENING THE BIBLE / by / THOMAS MERTON /
THE LITURGICAL PRESS / Collegeville, Minnesota
4 leaves, 1-84 pp., 2 blank leaves. 19 x 11½ cm. $3.75.
Light brown cloth, with Christian symbol, lettered in orange
on front cover. Light green end-papers. Pale green
dust-wrapper, with Christian symbol, printed in light
brown on front cover.
[Published in 1971.]

A59 *Contemplation in a World of Action* (1971)
a *First edition*:
CONTEMPLATION / IN A WORLD / OF ACTION /
[short horizontal line below title] / Thomas Merton /
INTRODUCTION BY JEAN LECLERCQ, O.S.B. /
1971 / Doubleday & Company, Inc., Garden City,
New York
3 leaves, [vii]-xxii, 1 leaf, [3]-384 pp., 1 blank leaf.
21½ x 14½ cm. $7.95. Brown cloth lettered downward
and across on spine in gold. Light brown end-papers.
Checkered brown and black dust-wrapper printed in grey
and white on front cover, downward and across on spine.
On verso of title-page: FIRST EDITION
[Published: February 26, 1971.]
Contents: INTRODUCTION BY JEAN LECLERCQ, O.S.B.—
EDITORIAL NOTE (by Naomi Burton)—One MONASTIC
RENEWAL—I Problems and Prospects—II Vocation and
Modern Thought—III The Identity Crisis—IV Dialogue and
Renewal—V Renewal and Discipline—VI The Place of
Obedience—VII Openness and Cloister—VIII Is the World a
Problem?—IX Contemplation in a World of Action—X The
Contemplative and the Atheist—XI Ecumenism and Renewal—
XII The Need for a New Education—XIII Final Integration:
TOWARD A "MONASTIC THERAPY"—Appendices—

1. NOTES ON THE FUTURE OF MONASTICISM—2. THE
MONK TODAY—Two THE CASE FOR EREMITISM—I
Christian Solitude—II The Cell—III Franciscan Eremitism—IV
The Spiritual Father in the Desert Tradition—V The Case of a
Renewal of Eremitism in the Monastic State—Three
CONTEMPLATIVE LIFE—Is the Contemplative Life Finished?

b *Paper-back edition*:
CONTEMPLATION / IN A / WORLD OF ACTION /
Thomas Merton / INTRODUCTION BY JEAN
LECLERCQ, O.S.B. / [publisher's symbol] / IMAGE
BOOKS / Garden City, New York / A Division of
Doubleday & Company, Inc. / 1973
    396 pp., 2 leaves. 18 x 11 cm. $1.95. Dark blue paper,
with design, printed in red and white on front cover
and downward on spine.
    On verso of title-page: Image Books edition published
February, 1973

A60 *Thomas Merton on Peace* (1971)
First edition:
    [Device] / THOMAS / MERTON / ON PEACE /
    [device] / With an Introduction by Gordon C. Zahn /
    The McCall Publishing Company / NEW YORK
    1 blank leaf, 3 leaves, [v]-xli, 1 leaf, [3]-269 pp.,
2 blank leaves. 22 x 15 cm. $7.95. Royal blue cloth with
design and TM imprinted in gold on front cover; spine
lettered across in gold; royal blue end-papers. Shaded blue
and white dust-wrapper printed in white and black on
front cover and downward on spine; back cover:
photograph of Thomas Merton, by John Howard Griffin.
    [Published: May 19, 1971.]
    Contents: Original Child Monk: An Appreciation, by Gordon C.
Zahn—Excerpts from Merton's following books: A38, A39,
A42, A45, A52, B42; included in this collection are twenty
articles appearing for the first time in book form: Preface to

Vietnamese Translation of No Man Is An Island—Peace and
Revolution: A Footnote from Ulysses—Christian Ethics and
Nuclear War—Christianity and Defense in the Nuclear Age—
Target Equals City—The Machine Gun in the Fallout Shelter—
Passivity and Abuse of Authority—A Martyr for Peace and
Unity—Auschwitz: A Family Camp—Danish Nonviolent
Resistance to Hitler—Saint Maximus the Confessor on
Nonviolence—Christian Action in World Crisis—Note on Civil
Disobedience and Nonviolent Revolution—Note for Ave Maria—
War and the Crisis of Language—Ishi: A Meditation—In
Acceptance of the Pax Medal, 1963—Retreat, November, 1964:
Spiritual Roots of Protest—Message aux Amis de Gandhi,
January 31, 1965—Notes for a Statement on Aid to Civilian War
Victims in Vietnam
    "Notes on Civil Disobedience and Nonviolent Revolution" was
submitted at the request of the National Commission on the
Causes and Prevention of Violence.

A61 *The Asian Journal of Thomas Merton* (1973)
First edition:
THE ASIAN JOURNAL / OF THOMAS MERTON /
[device] / Edited from his original notebooks / by
Naomi Burton, Brother Patrick Hart & James Laughlin /
Consulting Editor: Amiya Chakravarty / A NEW
DIRECTIONS BOOK
    3 leaves, vii-[xxx], 445 pp., 2 blank leaves. 23½ x 16 cm.
$12.50. Deep tan burlap cloth lettered downward in
iridescent blue on spine; deep tan end-papers. Beige
dust-wrapper, with design, printed in brown and blue
on front cover and downward on spine.
    42 photographs.
    [Published: July 16, 1973.]
    CONTENTS [:]—PREFACE—EDITORS' NOTES—
FOREWORD—PART ONE—The Eastward Flight / October
15-18—Calcutta / October 19-27—New Delhi / October 28-31—
The Himalayas / November 1-25—Madras / November 26-28—
Ceylon / November 29-December 6—Bangkok / December

B. Books with Contributions by Thomas Merton (Foreign and Domestic)

Arranged chronologically

B1 [A Brief Comment on Religious Poetry.] In a *New Anthology of Modern Poetry* (Revised Edition), edited, and with an Introduction, by Selden Rodman. New York: The Modern Library (December) 1946, p. 460. (A Modern Library Giant, ♯G 46.)

B2 "Foreword" (scattered excerpts: *The Seven Storey Mountain*). In *Burnt Out Incense*, by M. Raymond, O.C.S.O. New York: P. J. Kenedy & Sons (June) 1949, pp. xi, xii, xiii.

B3 "The Trappists Go to Utah" (see C15); "Poetry and the Contemplative Life" (see C14). In *The Commonweal Reader*, ed. Edward S. Skillin. New York, Harper & Brothers (September) 1949, pp. 13-20, 194-205.

B4 "An Introduction." In *The City of God*, by Saint Augustine. New York: The Modern Library (May) 1950, pp. ix-xv. (A Modern Library Giant, ♯G 74.)

B5 "The White Pebble" (see C50). In *Where I Found Christ*, ed. John A. O'Brien. New York: Doubleday & Company

(August) 1950, pp. 235-250. Also in *The Road to Damascus* (Volume II; A Pinnacle Book; same editor). London, W. H. Allen (no month) 1950, pp. 156-169.

B6 "Student, Man-About-the-Campus, Atheist, Trappist Monk" (excerpt: *The Seven Storey Mountain*). In *We Speak for Ourselves*, ed. Irving Stone. New York: Doubleday & Company (September) 1950, pp. [415]-421.

B7 [A Brief Comment.] (Back cover of dust-wrapper) for *The Pillar of Fire*, by Karl Stern. New York: Harcourt, Brace & Company (February) 1951. Also in paper-back. New York, Image Books, ♯ D83 (August, 1959); comment appears on recto of p. [1].

B8 "Thomas Merton / Seeds of Contemplation" (excerpt: *Seeds of Contemplation*). In *The Happy Crusaders* (A selection of readings affirming the joy of Christianity), compiled by James E. Tobin. New York: McMullen Books, Incorporated (April) 1952, pp. 107-110.

B9 "St. John of the Cross" (see C68). In *Saints for Now*, ed. Clare Boothe Luce. New York, Sheed & Ward (September) 1952, pp. 250-260 (plus 2 illustrations by Thomas Merton: St. John of the Cross and St. Therese of Lisieux, pp. 248, 280).

B10 "I Begin to Meditate" (see C30) (excerpt: *The Seven Storey Mountain*). In *The Catholic Digest Reader*, selected by the editors of The Catholic Digest. New York: Doubleday & Company (November) 1952, pp. [60]-65.

B11 "Saint Bernard, Moine et Apotre." In *Bernard de Clairvaux*, trans. J. de la Croix Bouton. Paris: Editions Alsatia (no month) 1953, pp. vii-xv.

B12 "August Seventh" (excerpt: *What Are These Wounds?*).
In *Christian Conversation* (*Catholic Thought for Every
Day in the Year*), ed. Anne Fremantle. New York:
Stephen Daye Press (November) 1953, p. [199].

B13 "The Contemplative Life Can Be Led By All" (excerpt:
Figures for an Apocalypse, from the essay *Poetry and
the Contemplative Life*). In a *Treasury of Catholic
Thinking*, compiled and edited by Ralph L. Woods.
New York: Thomas Y. Crowell Company (November)
1953, pp. 346-347.

B14 "Invisible Seeds; One's Own Virtues" (excerpt: *Seeds of
Contemplation*). In *The New Treasure Chest*, ed. J. Donald
Adams. New York: E. P. Dutton & Company
(November) 1953, pp. 409-410.

B15 "A Foreword" (see C74). In *St. Bernard of Clairvaux*,
newly translated and with an introduction by Rev.
Bruno Scott James. Chicago: Henry Regnery Company
(November) 1953, pp. [v]-viii.

B16 "The Primary Apostolate / The Apostolate of Prayer
and Penance." In *The National Catholic Almanac*
[50th Anniversary Edition], compiled by the Franciscan
Clerics of Holy Name College, Washington, D. C.
Paterson, New Jersey: Saint Anthony's Guild (January)
1954, pp. 343-344.

B17 " 'Truly a Success as a Cistercian' " (excerpt: *The Seven
Storey Mountain*). In *The Catholic Bedside Book* (*An
Anthology About Catholics and Catholicism*), general
editor: B. C. L. Keelan. New York: David McKay
Company, Incorporated (January) 1954, pp. 293-294.

B18 "Art Speaks to a Soul" (excerpt: *The Seven Storey
Mountain*). In *The Consolations of Catholicism*, compiled
and edited by Ralph L. Woods. New York: Appleton-
Century-Crofts, Inc. (November) 1954, pp. 106-107.

B19 "The Call of Silence" (excerpt: *Elected Silence, English*
version of *The Seven Storey Mountain*). In *Why I Became
a Priest*, ed. George L. Kane. Dublin: Browne & Nolan,
Limited (no month) 1954, pp. 18-32.

B20 "O Ultimo Padre da Igreja" (excerpt: *The Last of the
Fathers*). In *Perspectivas Dos Estados Unidos—
As Artes E As Letras*—trans. Adolfo Casais Monteiro.
Lisboa: Portugalia Editora (no month) 1955, pp. 265-301.

B21 [Scattered excerpts: *Seeds of Contemplation.*] In *The
American Treasury* (1455-1955), selected, arranged,
and edited by Clifton Fadiman, assisted by Charles Van
Doren. New York: Harper & Brothers (November)
1955, pp. 680-681.

B22 "The Trappists Go to Utah" (see B3, C15). In *The
Commonweal Treasury*, [which] is made up of selections
from the *Commonweal Reader* (see B3), ed. Edward S.
Skillin. New York: The Commonweal Publishing Co., Inc.
(December) 1955, pp. 116-123.

B23 "Preface." In *La Vie Eremitique*, by Paul Giustiniani.
Paris: Editions D'Histoire Et D'Art, Librairie Plon
(no month) 1955, pp. [7]-18.

B24 "In Silentio" [an introduction, trans. Marie Tadie].
In *Silence dans le Ciel*, a volume of ninety photographs of,
with captions by, the monks of La Pierre-qui-vire. This
is the First French Edition; the text and photographs are
scheduled to appear later under the title: *Silence in Heaven*

in England and America (see B27). Paris: Editions
Arthaud (4ᵉ trimestre), pp. 12-18, plus 58-59.
(The present edition appears both in cloth and paper.)

B25 "Preface." In *Seul avec Dieu: La Vie Eremitique*, d'apres
la doctrine du bienheureux Paul Giustiniani, by Dom
J. Leclercq. Paris: Librairie Plon (no month) 1955,
pp. 7-18.

B26 [Scattered excerpts: *Figures for an Apocalypse* (pp. 252,
328-329, 843); *The Seven Storey Mountain* (pp. 35,
109, 426, 837, 928); *Seeds of Contemplation* (pp. 92, 102,
213-214, 228, 259, 329, 342, 372, 381, 396, 422, 428,
435, 437, 453, 503, 602, 608, 617, 618, 629, 687, 713, 715,
721, 726, 774, 794, 819, 823, 831, 841, 876, 889, 902,
903-904, 929); *The Waters of Siloe* (pp. 59, 616-617, 619,
762); *The Ascent to Truth* (pp. 12, 329, 390, 411, 622);
The Sign of Jonas (p. 30); *The Living Bread* (pp. 166, 503,
629); *Poetry and the Contemplative Life* (see A5, B3,
C14) (pp. 34, 548, 690).] In *The Book of Catholic
Quotations*, selected and edited by John Chapin.
New York: Farrar, Straus and Cudahy (November) 1956.

B27 "In Silentio" [an introduction]. In *Silence in Heaven,
A Book of the Monastic Life* (see B24). New York:
The Studio Publications, in association with Thomas Y.
Crowell (no month) 1956, pp. 17-30.

B28 "The Pope of the Virgin Mary." In *Pio XII Pont. Max. /
Postridie Kalendas Martias / MDCCCLXXVI -
MDCCCCLVI. /* Rome, Italy: Typis Polyglottis Vaticanis
(no month) 1956, pp. 399-415.

B29 "The Cistercians and Carthusians" (excerpt: *The Waters
of Siloe*). In *A Treasury of Catholic Reading*, edited and
selected by John Chapin. New York: Farrar, Straus
and Cudahy (June) 1957, pp. [266]-273.

B30 " 'This Silence . . . The Room Jesus Told Us to Enter Into When We Pray' " (excerpt: *The Sign of Jonas*). In *A Treasury of the World's Great Diaries*, ed. Philip Dunaway and Mel Evans. New York, Doubleday and Company (no month) 1957, pp. [209]-217.

B31 "Selections From New Seeds of Contemplation." In *Come South Wind*, ed. M. L. Shrady. New York: Pantheon Books (no month) 1957, pp. 28-29, 40-41, 47-48, 57-58, 67.

B32 "A Life of Prayer" (an introduction, condensed from *A Balanced Life of Prayer*). In *A Catholic Prayer Book*, ed. Dale Francis. New York, A Dell Laurel Edition, published by the Dell Publishing Company (February) 1958, pp. [9]-12.

B33 " 'It was a Moment of Crisis . . . A Moment of Searching . . . A Moment of Joy' " (excerpt: *The Seven Storey Mountain*). In *Turning Point*, ed. Philip Dunaway and George de Kay. New York: Random House (no month) 1958, pp. [34]-38.

B34 "Solitude and Love." In *The Spirit of Man*, ed. W. Burnett. New York: Hawthorn Books (no month) 1958, pp. 113-119.

B35 [A Reading] (excerpt: *The Living Bread*). In *Devotions for Holy Communion*, revised and rearranged by Hubert McEvoy. Springfield, Illinois: Templegate Publishers (no month) 1959, pp. [242]-243.

B36 "Introduction." In *God Is My Life, The [Pictorial] Story of Our Lady of Gethsemani*; photographs by Shirley Burden. New York: Reynal & Company (no month) 1960, pp. [7-9]. (A portion of the text was written by Thomas Merton.)

B37 [A Letter.] In *The Lawson-Vanderbilt Affair* / *Letters to Dean Nelson* / *Excerpts from unsolicited letters* / *consequent upon the resigna-* / *tion of the Dean and eleven Fac-* / *ulty Members of the Divinity* / *School of Vanderbilt University.* / Privately Printed / Nashville, Tennessee: (August) 1960, p. 40.

B38 "Easter: The New Life." In *Harvest* / *1960*, ed. Dan Herr and Paul Cuneo. Westminster, Maryland: Newman Press (no month) 1960, pp. 159-170.

B38a "Poetry and Contemplation" (excerpt: *Selected Poems of Thomas Merton*; *A Thomas Merton Reader*; see C111). In *Essays in the American Catholic Tradition*, ed. Pierre Albert Duhamel. New York: Rinehart (no month) 1960, pp. 214-228.

B39 "Preface." In *Alone With God*, by Dom Jean Leclercq. New York: Farrar, Straus and Cudahy (July) 1961, pp. xiii-xxvii.

B40 "Preface." In *L'attente dans le silence*, by Dom M. Cheneviere. Paris: Desclee de Brouwer (no month) 1961, pp. 9-13.

B41 "Wisdom in Emptiness: A Dialogue by Daisetz T. Suzuki and Thomas Merton" (Prefatory Note); "Knowledge and Innocence"; "The Recovery of Paradise" (appeared in the Merton Reader); "Final Remarks" (pp. 65-101); the volume also contains brief biographical sketches of the poets represented and their poems which were translated by Thomas Merton; they are: "Drake in the Southern Sea" (in *Emblems of a Season of Fury*), by Ernesto Cardenal; "The Jaguar Myth"; "Cup with a Jaguar for the Drinking of Health"; "The Birth of

the Sun"; "The Despairing Man Draws a Serpent";
"The Secret of the Burning Stars"; "Pain is an Eagle
Clinging to Your Name"; "The Eye is a Dog Howling
in the Distance"; "Urn with a Political Profile";
"The World is a Round Earthenware Plate"; "Lament
of a Maiden for the Warrior's Death" (these poems are in
Emblems); "Faces of Girls Looking at Themselves in
the River"; "Meditation Before an Ancient Poem";
"Nahoa Urn, For a Woman"; "Written Next to a Blue
Flower," by Pablo Antonio Cuadra; the biographical sketch
of Jorge Carrera Andrade appeared in the *Merton Reader*
and *Emblems*; the poems of Andrade follow: "Cocoa Tree";
"The Weathercock on the Cathedral of Quito"; "A Man
From Ecuador Beneath the Eiffel Tower"; "The Mirror's
Mission"; "Notes of A Parachute Jumper" (these poems
are in *Emblems*); "Radicals" (pp. 102-123). In *New
Directions* 17, in *Prose and Poetry*, ed. James Laughlin.
New York: A New Directions Book (October) 1961.

B42 "Introduction" (pp. [7]-14); "Peace: A Religious
Responsibility" (pp. [88]-116). In *Breakthrough to
Peace / Twelve Views on the Threat of Thermonuclear
Extermination*. New York: A New Directions Paperbook
(September) 1962.

B42a "Poetry, Symbolism and Typology" (excerpt: *Bread
in the Wilderness*). In *Catholic Critics* (Volume 2),
ed. Philip Vitale. Chicago, Illinois: Auxiliary University
Press (no month) 1962, pp. 13-26.

B43 "Introduction" (excerpt: *Faith and Violence*). In
The Prison Meditations of Father Alfred Delp. New York:
Herder and Herder (no month) 1963, pp. vii-xxx. Also
in paper-back. New York: The Macmillan Company
(March) 1966, pp. vii-xxvi.

B44 "Preface." In *In Search of a Yogi*, by Dom Denys Rutledge. New York: Farrar, Straus and Company (April) 1963, pp. vii-xii.

B45 "Foreword." In *Notes on the Lord's Prayer*, by Raissa Maritain. New York: P. J. Kenedy & Sons (no month) 1964, pp. 7-11.

B46 "Atlas Watches Every Evening." In *New Directions* 18, ed. James Laughlin. New York: New Directions (no month) 1964, pp. 10-15.

B47 "A Devout Meditation in Memory of Adolf Eichmann." In *New Directions* 18, ed. James Laughlin. New York, New Directions (no month) 1964, pp. 16-18.

B48 "The Early Legend." In *New Directions* 18, ed. James Laughlin. New York: New Directions (no month) 1964, pp. 1-9.

B49 "Comments." In *War Within Man*, ed. E. Fromm. Philadelphia: Peace Literature Service of American Friends Service Committee (no month) 1964, pp. 44-50.

B50 "Foreword." In *Bernard of Clairvaux*, by H. Daniel-Rops. New York: Hawthorn Books (no month) 1964, pp. 5-7.

B51 "Reflections on the Character and Genius of Fenelon." In *Fenelon/Letters of Love and Counsel*, translated and selected by J. McEwen. New York: Harcourt, Brace & World (no month) 1964, pp. 9-30.

B51a "L'Evangile de la Misericorde." In *Hommage du Dr. Schweitzer*. Presente par Alphonse Goettmann. Paris: Les Editions du Cerf (no month) 1964, pp. 50-57.

64

B52 "Introduction." In *No More Strangers*, by Philip Berrigan. New York: The Macmillan Company (April) 1965, pp. [xi-xx]. Also in paperback. Techny, Illinois: Divine World Publications (May) 1967, pp. [ix]-xviii.

B53 "Introduction: Gandhi and the One-Eyed Giant." In *Gandhi on Non-Violence, Selected Texts from Mohandas K. Gandhi's Non-Violence in Peace and War*, ed. Thomas Merton. New York: A New Directions Paperbook (October) 1965, pp. 1-20.

B54 "Preface" (excerpt: *Faith and Violence*). In *Non-Violence and the Christian Conscience*, by P. Regamy. New York: Herder & Herder (no month) 1966, pp. 7-14.

B55 "Introduction." In *Religion in Wood*, by Edward D. & Faith Andrews, Bloomington, Indiana: Indiana University Press (no month) 1966, pp. vii-xv.

B56 "The Council and Monasticism." In *The Impact of Vatican II*, ed. Jude P. Dougherty. St. Louis, Missouri: B. Herder Book Company (no month) 1966, pp. 44-60

B56a "Day of a Stranger" (excerpt: *The True Solitude*; see C318, C350). In *The Borzoi College Reader*, ed. Charles Muscatine and Marlene Griffith. New York: Alfred Knopf (no month) 1966, pp. 661-667.

B57 [A Letter] (excerpt: *Faith and Violence*, entitled "Taking Sides on Vietnam"). In *Authors Take Sides on Vietnam*, ed. Cecil Woolf & John Bagguley. New York: Simon & Schuster (October) 1967, p. 51.

B57a "Foreword." In *The Mysticism of the Cloud of Unknowing: A Modern Interpretation*, by William Johnston. New York: Desclee and Company (no month) 1967, pp. ix-xiv.

B57b "Art; Morality." In the *New Catholic Encyclopedia* (Volume 1). New York: McGraw-Hill Book Company (no month) 1967, pp. 864-867.

B57c "Flannery O'connor." In *Les U.S.A. a la recherche de leur identité: Recontres avec 40 écrivains americains.* Pierre Dommergues, ed. Paris: Editions Bernard Grasset (no month) 1967, pp. 258-261.

B58 "Introductory Essay: 'Baptism in the Forest': Wisdom and Initiation in William Faulkner." In *Mansions of the Spirit*, ed. George A. Panichas. New York: Hawthorn Books (no month) 1967, pp. [19]-42.

B59 "Foreword." In *Vietnam: Lotus in a Sea of Fire* (translation of poems of Thich Nhat Hanh). New York: Hill & Wang (no month) 1967, pp. vii-x.

B60 "A Christian Looks at Zen." In *The Golden Age of Zen*, by J. C. Wu. Published by the National War College in cooperation with the Committee on the Compilation of the Chinese Library (no month) 1967, pp. 1-27.

B61 "Albert Camus and the Church." In *A Penny a Copy*, ed. Thomas C. Cornell & James H. Forest. New York: The Macmillan Company (no month) 1968, pp. 254-271.

B62 "Letter from Thomas Merton" (February, 1962). In *A Penny a Copy*, ed. Thomas C. Cornell & James H. Forest. New York: The Macmillan Company (no month) 1968, pp. 207-209.

B63 "Symbolism: Communication or Communion?" In *New Directions* 20, ed. James Laughlin. New York, *New Directions* (no month) 1968, pp. 1-15.

B64 "Letters to Che: Canto Bilinque." In *Viva Che!*
Contributions in Tribute to Ernesto "Che" Guevara,
ed. M. Alexandre. London: Lorrimer Publishers,
Limited (no month) 1968, p. 85.

B65 "The Significance of the Bhagavad Gita." In *The
Bhagavad Gita As It Is*, with Introduction, Translation
and Authorized Purport by A. C. Bhaktivedanta Swami.
New York: The Macmillan Company (November) 1968,
pp. [18]-22. Also in paperback. New York, Collier Books
(November) 1968, pp. [18]-22.

B66 "Morte D'urban: Two Celebrations." In *The Christian
Critic Series / J. F. Powers*, ed. Fallon Evans. St. Louis,
Missouri: B. Herder Book Company (no month)
1968, pp. [95]-100.

B66a "Excerpts from the New Man." In *Listen to Love:
Reflections on the Seasons of the Year*, comp. Louis M.
Savary. New York: Regina Press (no month) 1968,
pp. 143, 234.

B67 [A Letter.] In *Thomas Merton and the Story of a
Crucifix*, by Dr. Jose L. Morales. New York: New City
Press (no month) 1969, p. 1.

B68 "Learning to Live." In *University on the Heights*,
ed. Wesley First. New York: Doubleday & Company
(no month) 1969, pp. 187-199.

B69 "Plessy vs. Ferguson: Theme and Variations." In *New
Directions* 21, ed. James Laughlin. New York,
New Directions (no month) 1969, pp. 201-203.

B70 "Distractions in Prayer." In *Springs of Devotion*. Kansas
City, Missouri: Hallmark (no month) 1969, pp. 31-32.

B71 "Introduction." In *The Monastic Theology of Aelred of Rievaulx*, by A. Hallier. Spencer, Massachusetts: Cistercian Publications (no month) 1969, pp. vii-xiii.

B72 "War and the Crisis of Language." In *The Critique of War (Contemporary Philosophical Explorations)*, ed. Robert Ginsberg, Chicago: Henry Regnery Company (no month) 1969, pp. 99-119.

B72a "Purity" and "Death." In *Prophetic Voices: Ideas and Words on Revolution*, ed. Ned O'Gorman. New York: Random House (no month) 1969, pp. 164-172, 230-238.

B73 "Marxism and Monastic Perspectives." In *A New Charter for Monasticism*, by John Moffitt. Notre Dame, Indiana: University of Notre Dame Press (no month) 1970, pp. 69-81.

B73a "Excerpts from Various Works of Thomas Merton." In *Who Am I?: Second Thoughts on Man, His Loves, His Gods*, ed. Lowell D. Streiker. New York, Sheed and Ward (no month) 1970, pp. 9-10, 20, 25-26, 39-40, 51-52, 58, 83, 101-102, 108-110, 111-112, 116-117, 156-157, 165, 182, 204-205.

B73b "Light in Darkness: The Ascetic Doctrine of St. John of The Cross." In *Counsels of Light and Love of St. John of the Cross* (no editor given). Wheeling, West Virginia: Monastery of St. Teresa and St. John of the Cross of the Discalced Carmelite Nuns (no month, no year), pp. 9-20.

B74 "Monastic Experience and East-West Dialogue." In *The World Religions Speak on the Relevance of Religion in the Modern World*, ed. Finley P. Dunne, Jr. Netherlands, The Hague: Junk (no month) 1970, pp. 72-82.

B75 "Concerning the Collection in the Bellarmine College Library." In *The Thomas Merton Studies Center*, Volume One, by John Howard Griffin and Monsignor Horrigan. Santa Barbara, California: Unicorn Press (no month) 1971, pp. [13]-15.

B76 "Foreword." In *Psalms of Struggle and Liberation*, by Ernesto Cardenal, trans. Emile G. McAnany. New York: Herder and Herder (no month) 1971, pp. 7-8.

B77 "Introduction." In *To Live Is To Love*, by Ernesto Cardenal, trans. Kurt Reinhardt. New York: Herder and Herder (no month) 1972, pp. 7-18.

B78 "Openness and Cloister" (excerpt: *Contemplation in a World of Action*). In *Christian Readings*, Volume One. New York: The Catholic Book Publishing Company (April) 1972, p. 183.

B79 "The Discovery of Christ" (excerpt: *No Man Is an Island*); "Self-Denial and Sacrifice are Essential to the Life of Prayer" (excerpt: *Contemplative Prayer*). In *Christian Readings*, Volume Three. New York, The Catholic Book Publishing Company (April) 1972, pp. 193, 209.

B80 "The Modern World's Need for Mercy, Pardon, and Peace" (excerpt: *Conjectures of a Guilty Bystander*). In *Christian Readings*, Volume Four. New York: The Catholic Book Publishing Company (April) 1973, p. 169.

B81 "Search for God and Realism" (excerpt: *Life and Holiness*). In *Christian Readings*, Volume Five. New York: The Catholic Book Publishing Company (April) 1973, p. 47.

C. Contributions by Thomas Merton to Newspapers and Periodicals, Foreign and Domestic

Arranged chronologically

The following abbreviations are used: NYHTBR (New York Herald Tribune Book Review), and NYTBR (New York Times Book Review).

C1 [A review of] *The World's Body*. By John Crowe Ransom. *NYHTBR* (May 8, 1938) 10:2.

C2 [A review of] *Laughter in the Dark*. By Vladimir Nabokoff. *NYHTBR* (May 15, 1938) 10:2.

C3 [A review of] *The Enjoyment of Literature*. By John Cowper Powys. *NYHTBR* (November 20, 1938) 22:1.

C4 [A review of] *Defense of Art*. By Christine Herter. *NYHTBR* (December 25, 1938) 12:3.

C5 [A review of] *Romanticism and the Gothic Revival*. By Agnes Addison. *NYTBR* (January 29, 1939) 4:1.

C6 [A review of] *Plato Today*. By R. H. S. Crossman. *NYHTBR* (March 19, 1939) 15:1.

C7 [A review of] *John Skelton, Laureate*. By William Nelson. *NYTBR* (May 28, 1939) 2:2.

C8 [A review of] *The Personal Heresy*. By E. M. W. Tillyard & C. S. Lewis. *NYTBR* (July 9, 1939) 16:1.

C9 [A review of] *Religious Trends in English Poetry* (Vol. 1: 1700-1740). By Hoxie Neale Fairchild. *NYHTBR* (July 23, 1939) 17:2.

C10 [A review of] *The Burning Oracle*. By G. Wilson Knight. *NYTBR* (September 24, 1939) 5:2.

C11 [A review of] *D. H. Lawrence and Susan his Cow*. By William York Tindall. *NYTBR* (January 4, 1940) 4:1.

C12 "Huxley's Pantheon." *The Catholic World*, CLII. 908 (November 1940) [206]-209.

C13 [*Mystical Verse, a Letter*, by Thomas Merton.] *The Catholic Poetry Society of American Bulletin*, IV. 12 (December, 1941) 10. [Reply to Clara Hyde's letter in the *Bulletin*, IV. 11 (October, 1941) 4, in which she replied to "An Informal Editorial: Is Prayer Poetry" in the *Bulletin*, IV. 10 (August, 1941) 1.]

C14 "*Poetry and the Contemplative Life*" (see A5, table of contents in A32, a; B3). *The Commonweal*, XLVI. 12 (July 4, 1947) 280-286.

C15 "The Trappists go to Utah" (see B3). *The Commonweal*, XLVI. 20 (August 29, 1947) 470-473.

C16 "Death of a Trappist." *Integrity*, 2. 2 (November, 1947) 3-8.

C17 "The Trappists go to Utah" (condensed from *Commonweal*; see C15). The *Catholic Digest*, 12. 1 (November, 1947) 101-105.

C18 "Active and Contemplative Orders." *The Commonweal*, XLVII. 8 (December 5, 1947) 192-196.

C19 "A Christmas Devotion." *The Commonweal*, XLVII. 11 (December 26, 1947) 270-272.

C20 [A review of] *I Sing of a Maiden*. By Sister M. Therese. *The Commonweal*, XLVII. 19 (February 20, 1948) 477-478.

C21 "Death of a Trappist" (condensed from *Integrity*; see C16). *The Catholic Digest*, 12. 4 (February, 1948) 74-77.

C22 "A Trappist Speaks on People, Priests and Prayer." *The Messenger of the Sacred Heart*, LXXXIII. 4 (April, 1948) 58-61, plus 89-90.

C23 [A review of] *The Third Spiritual Alphabet*. By Fray Francisco de Osuna. *The Commonweal*, XLVIII. 4 (May 7, 1948) 85-86.

C24 "The Cause of Our Joy" (excerpt: *Cistercian Contemplatives*). *The Catholic World*, CXLVII. 1000 (July, 1948) 364-375.

C25 "Contemplation in a Rocking Chair." *Integrity*, 2. 11 (August, 1948) 15-23.

C26 "Schoolboy in England" (excerpt: *The Seven Storey Mountain*). *The Commonweal*, XLVIII. 20 (August 27, 1948) 469-471.

C27 "The Sweet Savor of Liberty" (excerpt: *The Seven Storey Mountain*). *The Commonweal*, XLVIII. 23 (September 17, 1948) 541-544.

C28 "One Sunday in New York" (excerpt: *The Seven Storey Mountain*). *Information*, LXII. 10 (October, 1948) 437-441.

C29 "Grace at Work" (excerpt: *The Seven Storey Mountain*; condensed from *Information*; see C28). *The Catholic Mission Digest*, VI. (November, 1948) 8-10.

C30 "I Begin to Meditate" (see B10) (excerpt: *The Seven Storey Mountain*). *The Catholic Digest*, 13. 1 (November, 1948) 116-120.

C31 "The Gift of Understanding." *The Tiger's Eye*, 6. 1 (December, 1948) 41-45.

C32 "I Begin to Meditate" (Japanese edition; see C30). *The Catholic Digest*, 2. 2 (February, 1949) 62-67.

C33 "Elected Silence" (excerpt: *Elected Silence*, English version of *The Seven Storey Mountain*) [in two issues]. [Part I] Foreword by Evelyn Waugh. *The Month*, 1. 3 (March, 1949) [158]-179; [Part II] 1. 4 (April, 1949) [221]-240.

C34 "Poverty" (excerpt: *Seeds of Contemplation*). *The Catholic Worker*, XV. 12 (April, 1949) 3:3.

C35 "Schoolboy's Lament" (excerpt: *The Seven Storey Mountain*). *The Catholic Digest*, 12. 8 (June, 1949) 80-82.

C36 "Peace That is War" (excerpt: *Seeds of Contemplation*). *The Liguorian*, XXXVII. 7 (July, 1949) 431.

C37 Page Proof (a brief excerpt: *The Waters of Siloe*). *The New York Post* (September 15, 1949) 30:1.

C38 "Is Mysticism Normal?" *The Commonweal*, LI. 4 (November 4, 1949) 94-98.

C39 "Trappists Make Silent Martyrs" (excerpt: *The Waters of Siloe*). *The Catholic Digest*, 14. 1 (November, 1949) 29-36.

C40 "The Contemplative Life / Its Meaning and Necessity." *The Dublin Review*, 446 (Winter 1949) 26-35.

C41 "First Christmas at Gethsemani" (unpublished material from the original ms. of *The Seven Storey Mountain*); introductory comment by Sister M. Therese Lentfoehr, S.D.S. *The Catholic World*, CLXX. 1017 (December, 1949) [166]-173.

C42 [An offprint of] The Transforming Union / in St. Bernard and St. John of the Cross. Extrait des—*Collectanea Ordinis Cisterciensium Reformatorum*—(in five issues) avril et juillet 1948, pp. [107]-117 et [210]-223; janvier et octobre 1949, pp. [41]-52 et [353]-361; janvier 1950, pp. [25]-38.

C43 "September, 1949" (later enlarged and included in *The Sign of Jonas*). *The Month*, 3. 2 (February, 1950) [107]-113.

C44 "Self-Denial and the Christian." *The Commonweal*, LI. 25 (March 31, 1950) [649]-653.

C45 "The Primacy of Contemplation." *Cross and Crown*, II. 1 (March, 1950) 3-16.

C46 "Todo y Nada / Writing and Contemplation" (unpublished material on Writing and Contemplation from the original ms. of *The Seven Storey Mountain*); introductory comment by Sister M. Therese Lentfoehr, S.D.S. *Renascence*, II. 2 (Spring 1950) 87-101.

C47 "Un Americano A Roma" (excerpt: *La Montagna Dalle Sette Balze*, Italian version of *The Seven Storey Mountain*). *L'Osservatore Romano* (28 April 1950) 3:2.

C48 "N.D. Gethsemani" [Chronique: Annual Report, Gethsemani; written in French] (Kentucky, Etats-Unis). *Collectanea Ordinis Cisterciensium Reformatorum*, XII. 2 (April, 1950) 132-134.

C49 "I Will be Your Monk" (unpublished material on St. Therese of the Child Jesus from the original ms. of *The Seven Storey Mountain*); introductory comment by Sister M. Therese Lentfoehr, S.D.S. *The Catholic World*, CLXXI. 1022 (May, 1950) [86]-93.

C50 "The White Pebble" (later enlarged and included in *Where I Found Christ*; see B5). *The Sign*, 29.12 (July, 1950) 26-28, plus 69.

C51 "The Psalms and Contemplation" [in three issues] (later enlarged and included in *Bread in the Wilderness*). *Orate Fratres* (now *Worship*), XXIV. 8 (July, 1950) 341-347; [Part II] XXIV. 9 (August, 1950) 385-391; [Part III] XXIV. 10 (September, 1950) 433-440.

C52 "Thomas Merton On Renunciation" (unpublished material from the original ms. of *The Seven Storey Mountain*); introductory comment by Sister M. Therese Lentfoehr, S.D.S. *The Catholic World*, CLXXI. 1026 (September, 1950) [420]-429.

C53 "Le Moine Et Le Chasseur." *Dieu Vivant*, 17 ([Fourth] Trimestre—1950), [93]-98.

C54 "Father Merton Denies Rumors." *The Catholic World*, CLXXII. 1032 (March, 1951) iv.

C55 "Monks and Hunters" (American version of *Le Moine Et Le Chasseur*; see C53. *The Commonweal*, LIV. 2 (April 20, 1951) 39-40.

C56 "N.D. Gethsemani" [Chronique: Annual Report, Gethsemani; written in French] (Kentucky, Etats-Unis). *Collectanea Ordinis Cisterciensium Reformatorum*, XIII. 2 (April, 1951) 141-142.

C57 "Etapes De Mon Chemin Vers Dieu" (excerpt: *La Nuit Privee D'Etoiles*, French version of *The Seven Storey Mountain*). *La Vie Spirituelle*, 365 (Août-Septembre 1951) [161]-171.

C58 "The Ascent to Truth" (excerpt: *The Ascent to Truth*). *Thought*, XXVI. 102 (Autumn 1951) [361]-383.

C59 "How to Believe in God" (excerpt: *The Ascent to Truth*). *The Catholic Digest*, 16. 3 (January, 1952) 41-44.

C60 "Christ Suffers Again." *Action Now!*, 5. 5 (March, 1952) 13.

C61 "N.D. Gethsemani" [Chronique: Annual Report, Gethsemani; written in French] (Kentucky, Etats-Unis). *Collectanea Ordinis Cisterciensium Reformatorum*, XIV. 2 (April 1952) [143]-144.

C62 "Le Sacrement De L'Avent / Dans La Spiritualite / De Saint Bernard." *Dieu Vivant*, 23 ([First] Trimestre—1953), [21]-43.

C63 Page Proof (a brief excerpt: *The Sign of Jonas*). *The New York Post* (February 5, 1953) 18:1.

C64 "The Sign of Jonas" (excerpt: *The Sign of Jonas*). *This Week Magazine* (March 8, 1953), 18, plus 30, plus 43, plus 50.

C65 "Les Psaumes Et La Contemplation" (French version of *The Psalms and Contemplation*; see C51). *Masses Ouvrieres*, 9. 85 (Avril 1953) 35-60.

C66 "Monastery at Midnight" (excerpt: *The Sign of Jonas*). *The Catholic Digest*, XVII. 7 (May, 1953) 112-116.

C67 "Saint Bernard: Monk and Apostle / Reflections in his Eighth Centenary Year" [in two issues]. *The Tablet*, 201. 5896 (May 23, 1953) 438-439; [Part II] 201.5897 (May 30, 1953) 466-467.

This article first appeared in French as the Preface to a biography of Saint Bernard, published by the Cistercian Order in commemoration of the eighth centenary of the saint's death. Frater Louis's superiors desired him to make an exception to his present practice of not writing for magazines in allowing this article to be printed here. It was also published in America; see C77.

C68 Page Proof (a brief excerpt: *Seeds of Contemplation*). *The New York Post* (June 16, 1953) 24:1.

C69 "St. John of the Cross." *Perspectives USA*, 4 (Summer 1953) [52]-61 (reprinted from Saints For Now; see B9).

C70 "St. John of the Cross." *Perspectives* (British edition; see C69], 4 (Summer 1953) [52]-61.

C71 "San Giovanni Della Croce." *Prospetti* [Italian edition; see C69], 4 (Summer 1953) [67]-76.

C72 "Der Heilige Johannes Vom Kreuz." *Perspektiven* [German edition; see C69], 4 (Summer 1953) [53]-62.

C73 "Saint Bernard Et L'Amerique" (excerpt: *Aux Sources Du Silence*, French version of *The Waters of Siloe*). [The first page of this article is new, the rest follows the text.] *Temoignages*, 38-39 (Juillet 1953) [89]-98.

C74 Page Proof (a brief excerpt: *Seeds of Contemplation*).
The New York Post (July 30, 1953) 20:1.

C75 "N.D. Gethsemani" [Chronique: Annual Report,
Gethsemani; written in French] (Kentucky, Etats-Unis).
Collectanea Ordinis Cisterciensium Reformatorum,
XV. 3 (July, 1953) 223.

C76 "Bernard of Clairvaux" (excerpt: A Forward, in *St.
Bernard of Clairvaux*; see B15). *Jubilee*, 1. 4 (August,
1953) 33.

C77 "St. Bernard, Monk and Apostle" (see footnote, C67).
Cross and Crown, V. 3 (September, 1953) 251-263.

C78 "The Psalms as Poetry" (excerpt: *Bread in the
Wilderness*). *The Commonweal*, LIX. 4 (October 30, 1953)
79-81.

C79 "O Diario De Thomas Merton" (excerpt: *The Sign of
Jonas*). *A Ordem*, L. 4 (outubro 1953) 17-25.

C80 Page Proof (a brief excerpt: *Bread in the Wilderness*).
The New York Post (December 22, 1953) 28:1.

C81 [An offprint of] "Action and Contemplation in St.
Bernard." Extrait des—*Collectanea Ordinis
Cisterciensium Reformatorum*—(in three issues)
janvier et juillet 1953, pp. [26]-31 et [203]-261;
avril 1954, pp. [105]-121.

C82 "N.D. Gethsemani" [Chronique: Annual Report,
Gethsemani; written in French] (Kentucky, Etats-Unis).
Collectanea Ordinis Cisterciensium Reformatorum,
XVI. 2 (April, 1954) [145].

C83 "Nel Deserto." *Camaldoli*, IX. 40 (Gennaio-Marzo 1955) 1-5.

C84 "Reality, Art, and Prayer" (excerpt: *No Man Is An Island*). *The Commonweal*, LXI. 25 (March 23, 1955) 658-659.

C85 "Dans Le Desert De Dieu." *Temoignages*, 48 (mars 1955) [132]-136.

C86 Page Proof (a brief excerpt: *No Man Is An Island*). *The New York Post* (March 28, 1955) 24:1.

C87 "You and I" (a brief excerpt: *No Man Is An Island*). *Books on Trial*, XIII. 6 (April, 1955) 311.

C88 "N.D. Gethsemani" [Chronique: Annual Report, Gethsemani; written in French] (Kentucky, Etats-Unis). *Collectanea Ordinis Cisterciensium Reformatorum*, XVII. 2 (April, 1955) [21].

C89 "Something to Live For" (a brief excerpt: *No Man Is An Island*). *NYTBR* (May 15, 1955) 2:5.

C90 Page Proof (a brief excerpt: *No Man Is An Island*). *The New York Post* (June 19, 1955) 8m:1.

C91 Page Proof (a brief excerpt: *No Man Is An Island*). *The New York Post* (June 21, 1955) 28:1.

C92 "Le Recueillement" (excerpt: *No Man Is An Island*). *Temoignages* (Juillet 1955) [321]-330.

C93 Page Proof (a brief excerpt: *No Man Is An Island*). *The New York Post* (August 29, 1955) 24:1.

C94 "Raccoglimento." *Camaldoli*, IX. 42 (Luglio-Settembre 1955) 81-88.

C95 "Praying the Psalms" (excerpt: *Praying the Psalms*). *Worship*, XXIX. 8 (September, 1955) 481-483.

C96 "The Tower of Babel" (excerpt: *The Strange Islands*; see A26). *Jubilee*, 3. 6 (October, 1955) [21-35].

C97 [An offprint of] "The Christmas Sermons of Blessed Guerric." Extrait des—*Collectanea Ordinis Cisterciensium Reformatorum*—(October-December 1955) [229]-244.

C98 "The Second Coming" (excerpt: *The Living Bread*). *Jubilee*, 3. 12 (April, 1956) [6]-9.

C98a "The Living Bread" (excerpt: *The Living Bread*). *Convivium*, I (1956) 27-32.

C98b "Two Meditations for the Members." *Convivium*, I (1956) 32-37.

C99 "Thomas Merton Notes on Sacred and Profane Art." *Jubilee*, 4. 7 (November, 1956) [25-32].

C100 "Time and the Liturgy" (excerpt: *Seasons of Celebration*). *Worship*, XXXI. 1 (December, 1956) 2-10.

C101 "Seeking God" (excerpt: *Basic Principles of Monastic Spirituality*). *Sponsa Regis*, 28. 5 (January, 1957) 113-121.

C102 [An offprint of] "La formation monastique selon Adam Perseigne." Extrait des—*Collectanea Ordinis Cisterciensium Reformatorum*, XIX (janv.-mars 1957) [1]-17.

C103 "Seeking Our Redeemer" (excerpt: *Basic Principles of Monastic Spirituality*). *Sponsa Regis*, 28. 6 (February, 1957) 141-149.

C104 "Sonship and Espousals." *Sponsa Regis*, 28. 7 (March, 1957) 169-178.

C105 "The Monk and Sacred Art." *Sponsa Regis*, 28. 9 (May, 1957) 231-234.

C105a "Preghiera al Sacro Cruore." *Convivium*, II (1957) 46.

C106 "The Pope of the Virgin Mary" (see B28). *Marian Literary Studies*, LXII (1958), 1-15.

C107 "Vision of Peace: Some Reflections on the Monastic Life." *Jubilee*, 6. 4 (August, 1958) [24]-27.

C108 "Lettre a un innocent spectateur" (excerpt: *The Behavior of Titans*). *Informations*, 77-78 (Août 1958) 29-31.

C109 [A brief comment re Boris Pasternak's *Doctor Zhivago*.] *The New York Times* (September 22, 1958) 29:4.

C110 " 'I Have Chosen You' " (excerpt: *Monastic Peace*). *Sponsa Regis*, 30. 1 (September, 1958) 1-6.

C111 "Poetry and Contemplation: A Reappraisal" (excerpt: *Selected Poems of Thomas Merton; A Thomas Merton Reader*). *The Commonweal*, LXIX. 4 (October 24, 1958) 87-92.

C111a "Carta a un espectador inocente" (excerpt: *The Behavior of Titans; Raids on the Unspeakable*). *Sur*, 256 (January-February 1959) 36-41.

C112 "Tribute to Greatness" [a comment re *Doctor Zhivago*]. *NYTBR* (February 1, 1959) 14:1.

C113 "The Secular Journals of Thomas Merton" (excerpt: *The Secular Journal of Thomas Merton*). *Jubilee*, 6. 10 (February, 1959) [16-20].

C114 "Ash Wednesday" (excerpt: *Seasons of Celebration*). *Worship*, XXXIII. 3 (February, 1959) 165-170.

C115 "Paques une vie Nouvelle." *La Vie Spirituelle*, 449 (avril 1959) [345]-359.

C116 "Easter: The New Life" (excerpt: *Seasons of Celebration*; see B38). *Worship*, XXXIII. 5 (April, 1959) 276-284.

C117 "Prayer for Guidance" [in art]. *Liturgical Arts*, 27. 3 (May, 1959) 64.

C118 "Christianity and Mass Movements." *Cross Currents*, IX. 3 (Summer 1959) [202]-211.

C119 "Spiritual Direction" (excerpt: *Spiritual Direction and Meditation*). *Sponsa Regis*, 30. 10 (June, 1959) 249-254.

C120 [A brief excerpt] *The Seven Storey Mountain*. *Reader's Digest*, 74. 446 (June, 1959) 26.

C121 "Boris Pasternak and the People with Watch Chains" (excerpt: *Disputed Questions*). *Jubilee*, 7. 3 (July, 1959) 19-31.

C122 "Esigenze Terrene e Mondo Migliore (Christianesimo e totalitarismo)" (excerpt: *Disputed Questions*). *Mondo Migliore*, V. 7 (Luglio 1959) [5-12].

C123 "Manifestation of Conscience and Spiritual Direction" (excerpt: *Spiritual Direction and Meditation*). *Sponsa Regis*, 30. 11 (July, 1959) 277-282.

C124 "Mount Athos" (excerpt: *Disputed Questions*). *Jubilee*, 7. 4 (August, 1959) 8-16.

C125 "Notas sobre arte sagrado y profano" (see C99). *Revista de Teologia*, VIII. 28-29 (Agosto 1959) 24-40.

C126 "Promethee" (excerpt: *Prometheus*). *La Revue Nouvelle*, XXX. 8-9 (Août-Septembre 1959) [145]-147.

C127 "Notes on Spiritual Direction" (excerpt: *Spiritual Direction and Meditation*). *Sponsa Regis*, 31. 3 (November, 1959) 86-94.

C127a "Boris Pasternak y los que llevan cadena de oro" (excerpt: *Disputed Questions*). *Sur*, 261 (November-December 1959) [9]-17.

C128 "Nativity Kerygma" (excerpt: *A Thomas Merton Reader*; *Seasons of Celebration*). *Worship*, XXXIV. 1 (December, 1959) 2-9.

C129 "Art and Worship." *Sponsa Regis*, 31. 4(December, 1959) 114-117.

C130 "My Visits to the Secular Bookhouse." *Staff Log* (Louisville Free Public Library), 24. 2 (December, 1959) 1-4.

C131 "Sacred Art and the Spiritual Life" (excerpt: *Disputed Questions*). *Sponsa Regis*, 31. 5 (January, 1960) 133-140.

C132 "What is Meditation?" (excerpt: *Spiritual Direction and Meditation*). *Sponsa Regis*, 31. 6 (February, 1960) 180-187.

C133 "The Ladder of Divine Ascent" (excerpt: *Disputed Questions*). *Jubilee*, 7. 10 (February, 1960) 37-40.

C134 "Meditation / Action and Union" (excerpt: *Spiritual Direction and Meditation*). *Sponsa Regis*, 31. 7 (March, 1960) 191-198.

C135 "Absurdity in Sacred Decoration" (excerpt: *Disputed Questions*). *Worship*, XXXIV. 5 (April, 1960) 248-255.

C136 "Presuppositions to Meditation" (excerpt: *Spiritual Direction and Meditation*). *Sponsa Regis*, 31. 8 (April, 1960) 231-240.

C137 "The Subject of Meditation" (excerpt: *Spiritual Direction and Meditation*). *Sponsa Regis*. 31. 9 (May, 1960) 268-274.

C138 "Temperament and Meditation" (excerpt: *Spiritual Direction and Meditation*). *Sponsa Regis*, 31. 10 (June, 1970) 296-299.

C139 "Le Mont Athos / Republique de la Priere" (excerpt: *Disputed Questions*). *Contacts (Revue Francaise de L'Orthodoxie*), 30 (2e Trimestre 1960), [92]-109.

C140 "St. Peter Damian and the Medieval Monk." *Jubilee*, 8. 4 (August, 1960) 39-44.

C141 "Herakleitos the Obscure" (excerpt: *The Behavior of Titans; A Thomas Merton Reader*). *Jubilee*, 8. 5 (September, 1960) [24]-31.

C142 "Love and Person." *Sponsa Regis*, 32. 1 (September, 1960) 6-11.

C143 "The Catholic and Creativity: Theology of Creativity" (excerpt: *A Thomas Merton Reader*). *The American Benedictine Review*, XI. 3-4 (September-December 1970) 197-213.

C144 "Let the Poor Man Speak!" *Jubilee*, 8. 6 (October, 1960) [18]-21.

C145 "Liturgy and Spiritual Personalism" (excerpt: *Seasons of Celebration*). *Worship*, XXXIV. 9 (October, 1960) 494-507.

C146 "Love and Maturity." *Sponsa Regis*, 32. 2 (October, 1960) 44-53.

C147 "A Signed Confession of Crimes Against the State" (excerpt: *The Behavior of Titans*). *The Carleton Miscellany* 1. 4 (Fall 1960) 21-23.

C148 "The Pasternak Affair in Perspective" (excerpt: *Disputed Questions*). *Thought*, XXXIV. 135 (Winter 1959-1960) [485]-517.

C149 "A Mountain of Monks" (excerpt: *Disputed Questions*). *The Catholic Digest*, 25. 2 (December, 1960) 100-103.

C150 "The Wisdom of the Desert" (excerpt: *The Wisdom of the Desert*; *A Thomas Merton Reader*). *Harper's Bazaar*, 2989 (December, 1960) [82]-85.

C151 "Classic Chinese Thought" (excerpt: *Mystics and Zen Masters*). *Jubilee*, 8. 9 (January, 1961) [26-32].

C151a "The Psalms" (excerpt: *Bread in the Wilderness*). *The Critic*, XIX. 4 (February-March 1961) 61.

C152 "The Person and Society" (excerpt: *Disputed Questions*). *Ave Maria*, 93. 9 (March, 1961) 27.

C153 "Original Child Bomb" (see A38, A60). *Pax* (1961) unpaged.

C154 "The Ox Mountain Parable of Meng Tzu." *The Commonweal*, LXXIV. 7 (May 12, 1961) 174.

C155 "Notes on Contemplation." *Spiritual Life*, 7. 3 (Fall 1961) 196-204.

C156 "The English Mystics" (excerpt: *Mystics and Zen Masters*). *Jubilee*, 9. 5 (September, 1961) 37-40.

C157 "The Root of War" (excerpt: *New Seeds of Contemplation*; *A Thomas Merton Reader*). *The Catholic Worker*, XXVIII. 3 (October, 1961) 1:5, 7:1, 8:1.

C158 "Miscellanea Monastica / The English Mystics. / In regard to some recent books." [Three essay-reviews of] *The English Mystical Tradition*, by David Knowles; *The Medieval Mystics of England*, edited, and with an introduction, by Eric Colledge; *Centuries of Meditations*, by T. Traherne. *Collectanea Cisterciensia*, XXIII. 4 (October-December 1961) [362]-367.

C159 "The Shelter Ethic." *The Catholic Worker*, XXVIII. 4 (November, 1961) 1:1, 5:2.

C160 "Called Out of Darkness" (excerpt: *The New Man*). *Sponsa Regis*, 33. 3 (November, 1961) 61-71.

C161 "The Testing of Ideals" (excerpt: *Life and Holiness*). *Sponsa Regis*, 33. 4 (December, 1961) 95-100.

C162 "The General Dance" (excerpt: *New Seeds of Contemplation*; *A Thomas Merton Reader*). *Jubilee*, 9. 8 (December, 1961) 8-11.

C163 "The Root of War" (see C157) (excerpt: *New Seeds of Contemplation*; *A Thomas Merton Reader*). *Fellowship*, 28. 1 (January 1, 1962) 5-11.

C164 "Christ, the Way" (excerpt: *Life and Holiness*). *Sponsa Regis*, 33. 5 (January, 1962) 144-153.

C164a "The Root of War" (see C157, C163) (excerpt: *New Seeds of Contemplation*; *A Thomas Merton Reader*). *Pax Bulletin* (London), 88 (January, 1962) 5-6.

C165 "Let the Poor Man Speak!" (reprinted from *Jubilee*, see C144). *The Catholic Mind*, LX. 1159 (January, 1962) 47-52.

C166 "Reflections on Grace and Free Will" (excerpt: *The New Man*). *The Tablet*, 216. 6349 (January 27, 1962) 79-80.

C167 "Man as God's Image and Likeness" (excerpt: *The New Man*). *The Tablet*, 216. 6350 (February 3, 1962) 102-103.

C168 "Nuclear War and Christian Responsibility." *The Commonweal*, LXXV. 20 (February 9, 1962) 509-513.

C169 "Man's Spirit in Bondage" (excerpt: *The New Man*). *The Tablet*, 216. 6351 (February 10, 1962) 127-128.

C170 "Life in Christ" (excerpt: *The New Man*). *The Tablet*, 216. 6352 (February 17, 1962) 151-152.

C171 "Itinerary to Christ." *Liturgical Arts*, 30. 2 (February, 1962) 70.

C172 "Thomas Merton on the Strike" [for peace] [a letter to Jim]. *The Catholic Worker*, XXVIII. 7 (February, 1962) 7:4.

C173 "A Letter to Pablo Antonio Cuadra Concerning Giants" (excerpt: *Emblems of a Season of Fury*). *Blackfriars*, XLIII. 500 (February, 1962) 69-81.

C174 "The Life of Faith" (excerpt: *Life and Holiness*). *Sponsa Regis*, 33. 6 (February, 1962) 167-171.

C175 "Growth in Christ" (excerpt: *Life and Holiness*). *Sponsa Regis*, 33. 7 (March, 1962) 197-210.

C176 [An editorial] "Christian Ethics and Nuclear War" (excerpt: *Thomas Merton on Peace*). *The Catholic Worker*, XVIII. 8 (March, 1962) 2:1, 7:1.

C177 "Red or Dead / The Anatomy of a Cliche." *Fellowship*, 28. 3 (March 1, 1962) 21-23.

C177a "Carta a Pablo Antonio Cuadra con respecto a los gigantes" (excerpt: *Emblems of a Season of Fury*; see C173, C186). *Sur*, 275 (March-April 1962) [1]-13.

C178 [An editorial] "Ethics and War / a Footnote." *The Catholic Worker*, XXVIII. 9 (April, 1962) 2:1.

C179 [A letter to Congressman Frank Kowalski (D. Connecticut) re Merton's supplication] A Prayer for Peace, Holy Week 1962, which was read by Mr. Kowalski in the House of Representatives (excerpt: *A Thomas Merton Reader*; *Thomas Merton on Peace*). *The Congressional Record*, Volume 108, Part 5 (April 18, 1962) 6937-6938.

C180 [Two letters re Nuclear War and Christian Responsibility] (see C168). The first was written by Joseph G. Hill and the second is Merton's reply. *The Commonweal*, LXXVI. 4 (April 20, 1962) 84-85.

C181 "Christian Culture Needs Oriental Wisdom" (excerpt: *A Thomas Merton Reader*). *The Catholic World*, 195. 1166 (May, 1962) [72]-79.

C181a "Red or Dead: The Anatomy of a Cliche" (see C177). *Pax Bulletin* (London), 89 (May, 1962) 6-8.

C182 "We Have to Make Ourselves Heard" [Part I] (excerpt: *Breakthrough to Peace* (see B42); *Thomas Merton on Peace*). *The Catholic Worker*, XXVIII. 10 (May, 1962) 4:1, 5:1, 6:4. (This article contains fragments of one that appeared in *The Commonweal* (see C168), revised and expanded.)

C183 "Religion and the Bomb" (excerpt: *A Thomas Merton Reader*). *Jubilee*, 10. 1 (May, 1962) [7]-13.

C184 "We Have to Make Ourselves Heard" [Part II] (excerpt: *Breakthrough to Peace* (see B42); *Thomas Merton on Peace*). *The Catholic Worker*, XXVIII. 11 (June, 1962) 4:1, 5:1.

C185 "Christian Action in World Crisis" (excerpt: *Seeds of Destruction*; *Thomas Merton on Peace*). *Blackfriars*, XLIII. 504 (June, 1962) 256-268.

C186 "Conquistador, Tourist, and Indian" (excerpt: *A Thomas Merton Reader*). *Good Work*, XXV. 3 (Summer 1962) 90-94. (This article is a revised version of *A Letter to Pablo Antonio Cuadra Concerning Giants*; see C173, C177a.)

C187 "Christian Freedom and Monastic Formation." *The American Benedictine Review*, XIII. 3 (September, 1962) 289-313.

C188 "The Jesuits in China" (excerpt: *Mystics and Zen Masters*). *Jubilee*, 10. 5 (September, 1962) 35-[38].

C188a "The Dance of Death." *Pax Bulletin* (London), 90 (September, 1962) 1-3.

C189 [A brief comment re Scripture.] *The New York Times Magazine* (October 14, 1962) 48:3.

C190 "Morte D'Urban: Two Celebrations" (see B66). *Worship*, XXXVI. 10 (November, 1962) 645-650.

C190a "Peril of Nuclear Hell Spurs Peace Seekers" (reprint of Thomas Merton's Introduction to *Breakthrough to Peace*; see B42). *The Los Angeles Times* (December 9, 1962) 1, 16-17.

C191 "Soldiers of Peace" (excerpt: *Clement of Alexandria*). *The Catholic Worker*, XXIX. 6 (January, 1963) 8:4.

C192 "Church and Bishop" (excerpt: *Seasons of Celebration*). *Worship*, XXXVII. 2 (January, 1963) 110-120.

C193 "Virginity and Humanism in the Latin Fathers" (excerpt: *Mystics and Zen Masters*). *Sponsa Regis*, 34. 5 (January, 1963) 131-144.

C193a "Thomas Merton Talks about the Small Rain." *The Spokesman* (Loras College, Dubuque, Iowa), LXI (1963) 50.

C194 "Hagia Sophia." *Ramparts*, 1. 5 (March, 1963) 65-71.

C195 "Pasternak" (excerpt: *Disputed Questions*). *The Catholic Worker*, XXIX. 8 (March, 1963) 7:5.

C196 "Martyr to the Nazis" (excerpt: *Introduction to The Prison Meditations of Father Alfred Delp*; see B43). *Jubilee*, 10. 11 (March, 1963) 32-35.

C197 "The Christian as Peacemaker" (excerpt: *Seeds of Destruction*). *Fellowship*, 29. 5 (March 1, 1963) 7-9.

C198 "Raissa Maritain's Poems." *Jubilee*, 10. 12 (April, 1963) 27.

C198a "Cuba Project: Letter to the Editor." *Liberation*, III (April, 1963) 30.

C199 "The Church in a Disillusioned World" (excerpt: *Introduction to The Prison Meditations of Father Alfred Delp*; see B43). *Way,* XIX. 4 (May, 1963) 4-10.

C200 "Zen: Sense and Sensibility." [A review of] *Zen Catholicism*, by Dom Aelred Graham. *America*, 108. 21 (May 25, 1963) 752-754.

C201 [A review of] *The Benedictines, a Digest for Moderns,* by
David Knowles, O.S.B. *Monastic Studies,* 1 (Pentecost
1963) 137-141.

C202 "Spirituality for the Age of Overkill." *Continuum,* I. 1
(Spring 1963) 9-21.

C202a "Christian Morality and Nuclear War." *Way,* XIV. 5
(June, 1963) 12-22.

C202b "Neither Caliban nor Uncle Tom." *Liberation,* VIII
(June, 1963) 20.

C203 "On Writing." *The Catholic Worker,* XXX. 1 (July-
August 1963) 6:2.

C204 "God is not Mocked" (excerpt: *New Seeds of
Contemplation*). *The Catholic Worker,* XXX. 3 (October,
1963) 6:4.

C205 "The Negro Revolt." [A review of] *A Different
Drummer,* by William Kelley. *Jubilee,* 11. 5 (September,
1963) 39-43.

C206 "Passivity and Abuse of Authority" (excerpt: *Thomas
Merton on Peace*). *Continuum,* I. 3 (Autumn 1963)
403-406.

C207 "A Homily on Light and on the Virgin Mother"
(excerpt: *Seasons of Celebration*). *Worship* XXXVII. 9
(October, 1963) 572-580.

C208 "Examination of Conscience and Conversatio Morum."
Collectanea Cisterciensia, XXV. 4 (October-December
1963) [355]-369.

C209 "Letters to a White Liberal" [Part I] (excerpt: *Seeds of Destruction*). *Blackfriars*, XLIV. 521 (November 1963) 464-477.

C210 "Letters to a White Liberal" [Part II] (Excerpt: *Seeds of Destruction*). *Blackfriars*, XLIV. 522 (December, 1963) 503-516.

C211 "The Advent Mystery" (excerpt: *Seasons of Celebration*). *Worship*, XXXVIII. 1 (December, 1963) 17-25.

C212 "The Black Revolution" (excerpt: *Seeds of Destruction*). *Ramparts*, 2. 3 (December, 1963) 4-23.

C212a [A letter to the editor.] *Eco Contemporaneo*, 6 / 7 (1963) 169-170.

C213 "Introducing a Book"; Introduction to Japanese edition of *The Seven Storey Mountain. Queen's Work*, 56.4 (January, 1964) 9-10.

C214 "The Shakers." *Jubilee*, 11. 9 (January, 1964) 37-41.

C215 "The Name of the Lord" (excerpt: *Seasons of Celebration*). *Worship*, XXXVIII. 3 (February, 1964) 142-151.

C215a "Ecclesiastical Baroque" (letter to the editor). [Reply to an article by James O'Gara; *The Commonweal, LXXIX*. 17 (January 24, 1964) 478.] *The Commonweal*, LXXIX. 19 (February 7, 1964) 573-574.

C216 "The Monk in the Diaspora" (excerpt: *Seeds of Destruction*). *The Commonweal*, LXXIX. 25 (March 20, 1964) 741-745.

C217 "Message to Poets" (excerpt: *Raids on the Unspeakable*). *El Corno Emplumado*, 10 (April, 1964) 127-129.

C218 "Message to Poets from Thomas Merton" (excerpt: *Raids on the Unspeakable*). *Americas*, XVI (May, 1964) 29.

C219 "To Each His Darkness" (excerpt: *Raids on the Unspeakable*). *Charlatan*, I (Spring 1964) unpaged.

C220 "The Council and Sacred Art" [Part I]. *Continuum*, 2. 1 (Spring 1964) 136-138.

C220a "The Black Revolution: Letters to a White Liberal" (see C209, C210, C212) (excerpt: *Seeds of Destruction*). *Albertus Magnus Alumna* I (Spring 1964) 8-13.

C221 "Truth and Violence." *Continuum*, 2. 2 (Summer 1964) 268-281.

C222 "The Council and Sacred Art" [Part II]. *Continuum*, 2. 2 (Summer 1964) 292-294.

C222a "Letter to the Editor." *The Blueprint* (Holy Angels Academy, Fort Lee, New Jersey), VII (June, 1964) 12-13.

C223 [A letter to the editor.] *El Corno Emplumado*, 11 (July, 1964) 154.

C223a "Letter to a Carmelite Nun on her Final Vows." *Review for Religious*, XXIII (July, 1964) 479-480.

C224 "The Monk in the Diaspora" (see C216) (excerpt: *Seeds of Destruction*). *Blackfriars*, XLV. 529-530 (July-August 1964) 290-301.

C225 "The 'Honest to God' Debate" (excerpt: *Faith and Violence*). *The Commonweal*, LXXX. 19 (August 21, 1964) 573-578.

C225a "The Extremists, Black and White: A Mystique of Violence." *Peace News* (September 18, 1964) 6:1.

C226 [A review of] *The Christian Commitment*. By Karl Rahner (excerpt: *Seeds of Destruction*). *Ramparts*, 3. 2 (October, 1964) 56-61.

C227 "Seven Qualities of the Sacred." *Good Work*, XXVII. 1 (Winter 1964) 15-20.

C228 "The Zen Revival." *Continuum*, I. 4 (Winter 1964) 523-538.

C229 [Four reviews of] *Christianisme russe*, by D. Barsotti; *English Spirituality*, by Martin Thornton; *Anglican Devotion*, by C. S. Stranks; *Honest to God*, by J. A. T. Robinson. *Collectanea Cisterciensia*, XXVI. 4 (October-December 1964) 333-335, 338, 338-339, 339.

C230 Three Letters. (To a Papal Volunteer, To a Brazilian Friend, To Dorothy Day; excerpt: *Seeds of Destruction*). *Motive*, XXV. 2 (November, 1964) 4-8.

C231 "Flannery O'Connor." *Jubilee*, 12. 7 (November, 1964) 49-53.

C232 "The Gentle Revolutionary" (excerpt: *Seeds of Destruction*). *Ramparts*, 3. 4 (December, 1964) 29-32.

C233 "Liturgical Renewal: The Open Approach" (excerpt: *Seasons of Celebration*). *The Critic*, XXIII. 3 (December, 1964) 10-15.

C233a [A review of] *The Story of Life*. By Konstantin Paustousky. *The Commonweal*, LXXXI. 11 (December 4, 1964) 358-359.

C234 "From Pilgrimage to Crusade" (excerpt: *Mystics and Zen Masters*). *Cithara*, IV (1964) 3-21.

C235 "The Humanity of Christ in Monastic Prayer." *Monastic Studies*, II (1964) 1-27.

C236 "Barth's Dream and Other Conjectures" (excerpt: *Conjectures of a Guilty Bystander*). *Sewanee Review*, LXXIII. 1 (1965) 1-18.

C237 "Mystics and Zen Masters" (excerpt: *Mystics and Zen Masters*). *Chinese Culture*, VI (1965) 1-18.

C238 "Le moine dans la Diaspora" (excerpts: *Seeds of Destruction*). *Bulletin de Liaison des Monasteres d'Afrique*, III (1965) 23-31.

C239 "Contemplation and Ecumenism" (excerpt: *Mystics and Zen Masters*). *Season*, III (1965) 133-142.

C240 "Answers on Art and Freedom" (excerpt: *Raids on the Unspeakable*). *The Lugano Review*, I (1965) 43-45.

C241 [A review of] *Varieties of Unbelief*, by Martin E. Marty (excerpt: *Faith and Violence*). *The Commonweal*, LXXXI. 15 (January 8, 1965) 490-491.

C242 [Eight reviews of] *The Spiritual Dialogue of East and West*, by J. A. Cuttat; *Zen, Weg zur Erleuchtung*, by H. M. Enomiya-Lasalle, S.J.; *The Matter of Zen / A brief Account of Zazen*, by Paul Wienpahl; *The Collected Works of Ramana Maharsi*, edited and annotated by Arthur Osborne; *One Hundred Poems* of Kabir, translated by Rabindranath Tagore, assisted by Evelyn Underhill; *Martin Lings, A Moslem Saint of the Twentieth Century*, by Shaikh Ahmad al'Alawi; *Three Muslim Sages, Harvard*

Studies in World Religions, by Seyyed Hossein Nasr; "*The Transformation of Man in Mystical Islam,*" by Fritz Meier, in *Man and Transformation, Papers from Eranos Yearbooks, Volume 5,* Bolligen Series XXX. *Collectanea Cisterciensia,* XXVII. 1 (1965) 77, 77-78, 78-79, 79-80, 80-81, 81-82, 83, 83-84.

C243 "Gandhi and the One-Eyed Giant" (excerpt: *Seeds of Destruction*). *Jubilee,* 12. 9 (January, 1965) [12-17].

C244 "Religion and Race in the United States." *New Blackfriars,* 46. 535 (January, 1965) [218]-225.

C245 "An Enemy of the State" (excerpt: *Faith and Violence; Thomas Merton on Peace*). [A review of] *In Solitary Witness,* by Gordon Zahn. *Peace News* (January 29, 1965) 5:1.

C246 [Three articles:] "The Function of a Monastic Review"; "For a Renewal of Eremitism in the Monastic State" (excerpt: *Contemplation in a World of Action*); "The Climate of Monastic Prayer" (excerpt: *Contemplative Prayer*). *Collectanea Cisterciensia,* XXVII. 1 (1965) 9-13, 121-149, 273-287.

C247 "The Challenge of Responsibility" (excerpt: *Seeds of Destruction*). *The Saturday Review,* XLVIII. 7 (February 13, 1965) 28-30.

C248 "A Tribute to Flannery O'Connor" (condensed from *Jubilee*; see C231). *The Catholic Mind,* LXIII. 1191 (March, 1965) 43-45.

C249 "Barth's Dream" (excerpt: *Conjectures of a Guilty Bystander*). *Motive,* XXV. 6 (March, 1965) back cover of magazine.

C249a "Is Man a Gorilla with a Gun?" (excerpt: *Faith and Violence*; *Thomas Merton on Peace*). [A review of] *African Genesis*, by Robert Ardrey. *Negro Digest*, XIV. 5 (March, 1965) 8-14.

C250 "The Climate of Mercy." *The Cord*, XV. 4 (April, 1965) 89-96.

C251 "Pacifism and Resistance" (excerpt: *Faith and Violence*; *Thomas Merton on Peace*). [A review of] *Simone Weil (a Fellowship in Love)*, by Jacques Cabaud. *Peace News* (April 2, 1965) 5:1, 8:1.

C252 [A letter re "The Council and the Bomb," by James Douglass (*The Commonweal*, LXXXI. 23 (March 5, 1965) 725-728).] *The Commonweal*, LXXXII. 2 (April 2, 1965) 62-63.

C253 "A Priest and his Mission." *Continuum*, 3. 1 (Spring 1965) 126-130.

C254 "Rain and the Rhinoceros" (excerpt: *Raids on the Unspeakable*). *Holiday*, 37. 5 (May, 1965) 8-16.

C254a "An Enemy of the State" (excerpt: *Faith and Violence*; *Thomas Merton on Peace*). [A review of] *In Solitary Witness*, by Gordon Zahn. *Pax Bulletin* (London), 97 (May, 1965) 3-4.

C255 "Man is a Gorilla with a Gun: Reflections on an American Best Seller" (see C249a) (excerpt: *Faith and Violence*; *Thomas Merton on Peace*). [A review of] *African Genesis*, by Robert Ardrey. *New Blackfriars*, XLVI. 539 (May, 1965) 452-457.

C255a "Vietnam and Pacifism" (a letter to the editor). [Reply to two letters: "Pacifism of the Weak," by James

Forest; "Pacifism and Vietnam," by Charles A. Knight. *The Commonweal*, LXXXII. 4 (April 16, 1965) 99, 125-126, 126-127.] *The Commonweal*, LXXXII. 7 (May 7, 1965) 202.

C255b "The Brothers and Aggiornamento." *The Brothers Newsletter*, VII (Summer 1965) 8-10.

C256 "Reflections on Some Recent Studies of Saint Anselm." *Monastic Studies*, 3 (Feast of St. Benedict 1965) 221-234.

C257 [A review of] *Ascetismo e Monachesimo Prebenedittino*. By Giuseppe Turbessi. *Monastic Studies*, 3 (Feast of St. Benedict 1965) 269-271.

C258 "The Night Spirit and the Dawn Air" (excerpt: *Conjectures of a Guilty Bystander*). *New Blackfriars*, 46. 543 (September, 1965) 687-693.

C259 "The Poorer Means." *The Cord*, XV. 9 (September, 1965) 243-247.

C260 "The Place of Obedience in Monastic Renewal" (excerpt: *Contemplation in a World of Action*). *The American Benedictine Review*, XVI. 3 (September, 1965) 359-368.

C261 "An Open Letter to the American Hierarchy (Schema XIII and the Modern Church)." *Worldview*, 8. 9 (September, 1965) 4-6.

C262 "St. Maximus: The Confessor on Nonviolence" (excerpt: *Thomas Merton on Peace*). *The Catholic Worker*, XXXII. 1 (September, 1965) 1:2, 2:3.

C263 "The Contemplative Life in the Modern World" (excerpt: *Faith and Violence*). *The Mountain Path* (October, 1965) [223]-227.

C264 "The Council and Religious Life." *New Blackfriars*, 47. 544 (October, 1965) 5-17.

C264a "Truth and Crisis: Pages from a Monastic Notebook" (excerpt: *Conjectures of a Guilty Bystander*). *Gandhi Marg* (India), IX (October, 1965) 294-298.

C264b "The Christian in Time of Change." *The Rambler* (Ladycliff College, Highland Falls, New York), X (October 15, 1965) 1.

C264c "Contemplation and Ecumenism." *Season*, III (Fall 1965) 133-142.

C265 "Mensaje a los poetas" (see C217, C218) (excerpt: *Raids on the Unspeakable*). *Eco Contemporaneo*, 8/9 (Invierno 1965) 60-62.

C266 "The Other Side of Despair: Notes on Christian Existentialism" (excerpt: *Mystics and Zen Masters*). *The Critic*, XXIV. 2 (October, 1965) 13-23.

C267 [Two letters re] "An Open Letter to the American Hierarchy" (see C261), by Thomas Molnar and Thomas Merton's reply to Molnar. *Worldview*, 8. 11 (November, 1965) 11-13.

C268 "Il concilio e la vita dei religiosi" (see C264). *Humanitas*, XX. 11 (Novembre 1965) [1097]-1115.

C269 "Few Questions and Fewer Answers: extracts from a Monastic Notebook" (excerpt: *Conjectures of a Guilty Bystander*). *Harper's Magazine*, 231. 1386 (November, 1965) [79]-81.

C270 "The Time of the End is the Time of no Room"
(excerpt: *Raids on the Unspeakable*). *Motive*, XXVI.
3 (December, 1965) 4-9.

C271 "The Good News of the Nativity." *The Bible Today*,
21 (December, 1965) 1367-1375.

C271a "Schema XIII: An Open Letter to the American
Hierarchy" (see C261, C267). *Vox Regis* (Christ the King
Seminary, Saint Bonaventure, New York), XXXI
(December, 1965) 5-7.

C272 [A review of] *The Call of the Desert*, by Peter F. Anson;
"Tradition Occidentale/S. Augustin" [a review of
Saint Augustine as Psychotherapist, by Martin Versfeld,
in *Blackfriars*, XLV (1964) 98-110]; [a brief summary of]
*L'art irlandais, Photographies inedites de Pierre Belzaux,
nombreuses planches en couleurs et cartes*, by Francoise
Henry. *Collectanea Cisterciensia*, XXVII. 4 (1965)
(*Bulletin De Spiritualite Monastique*) (1965) (♯ 1, 2 & 3)
257-258, 302-303, 324.

C273 "La place de l'obeisance dans la renouveau monastique"
(a French translation of: *The Place of Obedience in
Monastic Renewal*; see C260) (excerpt: *Contemplation
in a World of Action*). *Lettre de Liguge*, CXIX
(1966) 8-19.

C274 "The Zen Koan" (excerpt: *Mystics and Zen Masters*).
The Lugano Review, 1 (1966) 126-139.

C274a "Comments on Doctor Prince's and Doctor Savage's
Paper on Mystical States and Regression." *Newsletter-
Review* (The R. M. Bucke Memorial Society, Montreal),
1 (January, 1966) 4-5.

C275 "No More Strangers" (excerpt: *Introduction*; see B52). *The Catholic Worker*, XXXII. 6 (February, 1966) 5:1.

C275a "Holy Camp." [A review of] *Monks, Nuns, and Monasteries*. By Sackeverell Stitwell. *The Critic*, XXIV. 4 (February-March 1966) 68-70.

C276 [A review of] *In Tune With the World, a Theory of Festivity*. By Josef Pieper, trans. Richard and Clara Winston. *Cistercian Studies*, I. 1 (1966) 108-109.

C277 "Conversatio Morum." *Cistercian Studies*, I. 2 (1966) 130-144.

C277a "The Meaning of Satyagraha." *Gandhi Marg* (India), X (April, 1966) 108-110.

C277b "La otra para de la desesperacion (notas sobre el existencialismo Cristiano)" (see C266) (excerpt: *Mystics and Zen Masters*). *Sur*, 300 (May-June 1966) [29]-46.

C278 "St. Anselm and his Argument." *The American Benedictine Review*, XVII. 2 (June, 1966) 238-262

C279 "Is the World a Problem?" (excerpt: *Contemplation in a World of Action*). *The Commonweal*, LXXXIV. 11 (June 3, 1966) 305-309.

C280 "Events and Pseudo-Events: Letter to a Southern Churchman" (excerpt: *Faith and Violence*). *Katallagete* (Summer 1966) 10-17.

C281 "Nhat Hanh Is My Brother" (excerpt: *Faith and Violence*; *Thomas Merton on Peace*). *Jubilee*, 14. 4 (August, 1966) 11.

C282 "Conjectures of a Guilty Bystander" (excerpt:
Conjectures of a Guilty Bystander). *Life*, 61. 6 (August 5,
1966) 60-62, 64-66, 68, 71-73.

C283 "Ruben Dario." *Continuum*, IV. 3 (1966) 469-470.

C283a "Transcendent Experience." *Newsletter-Review*
(The R. M. Bucke Memorial Society, Montreal), 1
(September, 1966) 5.

C284 "Buddhism and the Modern World" (excerpt:
Mystics and Zen Masters). *Cross Currents*, XVI.
4 (Fall 1966) 495-499.

C285 "Symbolism: Communication or Communion?"
(see B63). *The Mountain Path* (October, 1966)
[339]-348.

C286 "A Devout Meditation on Adolf Eichmann" (see B47)
(excerpt: *Raids on the Unspeakable*; *Thomas Merton
on Peace*). Ramparts, 5. 4(October, 1966) 8-10.

C287 "Love and Solitude." *The Critic*, XXV. 2 (October-
November 1966) 31-37.

C288 "A Meditation on Adolf Eichmann" (see B47, C286)
(excerpt: *Raids on the Unspeakable*; *Thomas Merton
on Peace*). *The Catholic Digest*, 31. 1 (November,
1966) 18-20.

C289 "Peace and Protest" (excerpt: *Faith and Violence*).
Continuum, 3. 4 (Winter 1966) 509-512.

C290 "How It Is/Apologies to an Unbeliever" (excerpt:
Faith and Violence). *Harper's Magazine*, 233.
1398 (November, 1966) 36-39.

C291 "Monastic Vocation and Modern Thought" (excerpt: *Contemplation in a World of Action*). *Monastic Studies*, 4 (Advent 1966) 17-54.

C292 "Orthodoxy and the World." *Monastic Studies*, 4 (Advent 1966) 105-115.

C293 [Six reviews of] *Anselme von Canterbury*, by Leo Helbling, O.S.B.; *L'utilisation de l'Écriture Sainte chez Anselme de Cantorbery*, by R. Gregoire, O.S.B.; *La Recitudo chez saint Anselme/Un itinéraire augustinien de l'am à Dieu*, by Robert Pouchet; *Seraphim vom Sarow*, by Vera Zander; *Lo doctrine spirituelle de Theophane le Reclus*, by Thomas Spidlik, S.J.; *Écrits spirituels, presentation d'Edouard Duperrary*, by Jules Monachanin. *Collectanea Cisterciensia*, XXVIII. 4 (1966) (*Bulletin De Spiritualité Monastique*) (1966) (♯ 4 & 5) 321, 321-322, 322-323, 345, 346-347, 361-362.

C294 [Three comments re] *Le Meditations del Beato Guigo Certosino*, by Maria-Elena Cristofolini, in *Aevum* 39 (1965) 201-217; *Anselme De Havelberg, Dialogues I, texte Latin, notes* et trad. par Gaston Salet, S.J. (*Sources Chretiennes* 118, *textes monastiques d'Occident* 18); *Noticias acerca de la vida eremitica en Hispano-America*, by Mauro Matthei, in *Yermo* 3 (1965) 171-188. *Collectanea Cisterciensia*, XXVIII. 4 (1966) (*Bulletin De Spiritualité Monastique*) (1966) (♯ 4 & 5) 324, 335, 353.

C295 "A Buyer's Market for Love?" *Ave Maria*, 104. 26 (December 24, 1966) 7-10, plus 27.

C296 "Albert Camus and the Church" (see B61). *The Catholic Worker*, XXXIII. 3 (December, 1966) 1:1, 4:1, 5:1, 8:3.

C297 "Franciscan Eremitism" (excerpt: *Action in a World of Contemplation*). *The Cord*, XVI. 12 (December, 1966) 356-364.

C298 "Thomas Merton Replies to a Perceptive Critic." *The National Catholic Reporter*, 3. 12 (January 18, 1967) 4:5. [The letter is a reply to Michele Murray who reviewed *Conjectures of a Guilty Bystander* and *Raids on the Unspeakable* (December 21, 1966).]

C299 "Moines et Spirituels non Chretiens II." [Nine reviews of] *Final Integration in the Adult Personality*, by A. Reza Arasteh; *The Kingdom of God Today*, by Otto Karrer; *Spiritual Consciousness in Zen from a Thomistic Theological Point of View*, by Rev. Augustin Hideshi Kishi; *Zen and Christian Mysticism*, by William Johnston; *Technique and Personal Devotion in the Zen Exercise*, by Heinrich Dumoulin, S.J.; *The Awakening of a New Consciousness in Zen*, by Daisetz Teitaro Suzuki; *Life is Tragic: The Diary of Nishida Kitaro*, by Lothar Knauth; *A Study of Good*, by Nishida Kitaro; *Zen in Japanese Art: A Way of Spiritual Experience*, by Toshimitsu Hasumi. *Collectanea Cisterciensia*, XXIX. 1 (1967) 179-190.

C300 [A review of] *The Mystical Consciousness and World Understanding*, by Walter Houston Clark, in the *Journal for the Scientific Study of Religion*, IV. 2 (Printemps 1965) *Collectanea Cisterciensia*, XXIX. 1 (1967) 191-192.

C301 [A summary re an] Editorial in the *Psychedelic Review*, 6 (1965). *Collectanea Cisterciensia*, XXIX. 1 (1967) 192-194.

C302 [Two reviews of] *Partir au desert*, by Peter F. Anson; *Hesychasme et priere*, by I. Hausherr. *Collectanea Cisterciensia*, XXIX. 1 (1967) (*Bulletin De Spiritualité Monastique*) (1967) (♯ 1) 19-20, 21-22.

C303 [Four comments re] *Monasterium-carcer*, by Gregorio Penco, in *SM* 8 (1966) 133-143; *Los monasterios de monjan en Galicia*, by German Martinez, in *Yermo* 4 (1966) 51-78; *Les chretientes celtiques*, by Olivier Loyer; *The Dream of the Rood and Anglo-Saxon Monasticism*, by John Fleming, in *Traditio* 22 (1966) 43-72. *Collectanea Cisterciensia*, XXIX. 1 (1967) (*Bulletin De Spiritualité Monastique*) (1967) (♯ 3) 66, 77, 78-79, 80.

C304 [Six reviews of] *Saint Bruno*, by Andre Ravier, S.J.; *The Grandmontines*, by Desmond Seward, in *The Downside Review* 83 (1965) 249-264; *Los monasterios de Benedictinos de Galicia*, by Maximino Arias, in *SM* 8 (1966) 35-69; *Isaac De L'Etoile, Sermons, t. I*. Texte et introduction critiques par Anselme Hoste, O.S.B., introduction, traduction et notes par Gaston Salet, S.J. (Coll. *Sources Chretiennes* 130, *Serie des textes monastiques d'Occident* 20) ; *Gertrude D'Helfta, Oeuvres spirituelles, t. I. Les exercices*. Texte Latin, introduction, traduction et notes par Jacques Hourlier et Albert Schmitt. (Coll. *Sources Chretiennes* 127, *Serie des textes monastiques d'Occident* 19) ; *L'eremitisme a la Catalunya nova*, by E. Fort Cogul, in *SM* 7 (1965) 63-126. *Collectanea Cisterciensia*, XXIX. 1 (1967) (*Bulletin De Spiritualité Monastique*) (1967) (♯ 4) 88, 88-89, 89, 103-104, 107, 109-110.

C305 "Monachisme Bouddhique: Le Zen" (excerpt: *Mystics and Zen Masters*). *Collectanea Cisterciensia*, XXIX. 1 (1967) 132-150.

C306 "Monastic Attitudes: A Matter of Choice." *Cistercian Studies*, II. 1 (1967) 3-14.

C307 [Three reviews of] *Mallorca eremitica, por un Ermitano*, Imp. Sagrados Corazones; *Monasterios y monjes en los (Diarios de Jovellanos)*, by I. M. Gomez, in *Yermo* 4 (1966) 107-213; *Un manual de ermitanos*, by Garcia M. Colombas, O.S.B., in *Yermo* 3 (1965) 317-333. *Collectanea Cisterciensia*, XXIX. 1 (1967) (*Bulletin De Spiritualité Monastique*) (1967) (♯ 5) 116-117, 122, 127-128.

C308 [Two essay-reviews of] *Christ in the Wilderness*, by Ulrich Mauser, *Wilderness and Paradise in Christian Thought*, by George H. Williams. *Cistercian Studies*, II. 1 (1967) 83-89.

C309 "The Death of God and the End of History" (excerpt: *Faith and Violence; Thomas Merton on Peace*). *Theoria to Theory*, II (1967) 3-16.

C310 "Christian Solitude: Notes on an Experiment" (excerpt: *Contemplation in a World of Action*). *The Current*, IX (February, 1967) 76-80.

C311 "The True Legendary Sound." *Sewanee Review*, LXXV. 2 (1967) 317-324.

C311a "Paradise Bugged." [A review of] *All: The Collected Short Poems* (1956-1964), by Louis Zukofsky. *The Critic*, XXV. 4 (February-March 1967) 69-71.

C311b "Mississippi y Auschwitz." *La Liberacion por la Nonviolencia*, IV (Marzo 1967) 3-4.

C312 "Ishi: A Meditation" (excerpt: *Thomas Merton on Peace*). [A review of] *Ishi in Two Worlds: A Biography*

of the last wild Indian in North America. By Theodora
Kroeber. *The Catholic Worker*, **XXXIII**. 6 (March-April
1967) 5:1, 6:5.

C313 [A brief excerpt: *Conjectures of a Guilty Bystander.*]
The Saturday Review, L. 15 (April 15, 1967) 11.

C314 "Can We Survive Nihilism?" *The Saturday Review*,
L. 15 (April 15, 1967) 16-19.

C314a "The Self of Modern Man and the New Christian
Consciousness." *Newsletter-Review* (The R. M. Bucke
Memorial Society, Montreal), II (April, 1967) 1-7.

C314b "Notes on Prayer and Action." *The Light*,
I (April-May 1967) 1, 3.

C315 "The Sounds are Furious." [A review of] *Faulkner:
A Collection of Critical Essays*. Ed. Robert Penn Warren.
The Critic, **XXV** (April-May 1967) 76-80.

C316 "Blessed are the Meek: The Christian Roots of
Nonviolence" (excerpt: *Faith and Violence*; *Thomas
Merton on Peace*). *Fellowship*, 33. 5 (May, 1967) 18-22.

C317 "A Devout Meditation in Memory of Adolf Eichmann"
(see B47, C286, C288) (excerpt: *Raids on the Unspeakable*;
Thomas Merton on Peace). *Peace News*
(May 19, 1967) 12:1.

C317a "D. T. Suzuki (el hombre y su obra)" (excerpt:
Zen and the Birds of Appetite). *Sur*, 306
(May-June 1967) [26]-31.

C318 "Day of a Stranger" (excerpt: *The True Solitude*).
The Hudson Review, **XX**. 2 (Summer 1967) [211]-218.

C319 "The Church in World Crisis." *Katallagete*
(Summer 1967) 30-36.

C320 "The Meaning of Malcolm X" (excerpt: *Faith and Violence*). *Continuum*, 5. 2 (Summer 1967) 432-435.

C321 [A review of] *The Shoshoneans*. By Edward Dorn.
The Catholic Worker, XXXIII. 8 (June, 1967) 5:1, 6:1.

C322 "The Death of a Holy Terror/The Strange Story of
Frère Pascal." *Jubilee*, 15. 2 (June, 1967) 35-[38].

C322a "The Zen Koan" (see C274) (excerpt: *Mystics and Zen Masters*). *Retort* (Birmingham University Chemical Society), XLII (June, 1967) 9-16.

C322b "Ishi: A Meditation" (see C312) (excerpt: *Thomas Merton on Peace*). [A review of] *Ishi in Two Worlds: A Biography of the last wild Indian in North America.*
By Theodora Kroeber. *Peace News* (June 30, 1967)
6:1, 7:1.

C323 "Zukofsky: The Paradise Ear" (see C311a). [A review of] *All: The Collected Short Poems, 1956-1964.*
By Louis Zukofsky. *Peace News* (July 28, 1967) 8:1.

C323a "Blessed are the Meek: The Christian Roots of
Nonviolence" (see C316) (excerpt: *Faith and Violence; Thomas Merton on Peace*). *Gandhi Marg* (India),
XI (July, 1967) 232-240.

C324 [A review of] *Zen in Japanese Art: A Way of Spiritual Experience.* By Toshimitsu Hasumi. *The Catholic Worker*,
XXXIII. 9 (July-August 1967) 8:4.

C325 "Original Child Bomb" (see A38, A60). *Peace News*
(August 4, 1967) 6:1.

C326 [A review of] *From Primitives to Zen, a Thematic Sourcebook on the History of Religions*. By M. Eliade. The National Catholic Reporter, 3. 42 (August 23, 1967) 9:2.

C326a "D. T. Suzuki: The Man and his Work" (see C317a) (excerpt: *Zen and the Birds of Appetite*). *Eastern Buddhist*, II (August, 1967) 1-5.

C327 "Rafael Alberti and his Angels." *Continuum*, 5. 1 (September, 1967) 175-179.

C328 "Sincerity in Art and Life." *Good Work*, XXX. 2 (September, 1967) 58-59.

C329 "Isaac of Stella/An Introduction to Selections from his Sermons." *Cistercian Studies*, II. 3 (1967) 243-251.

C330 "Negro Violence and White Non-Violence." [A letter to Dr. Martin E. Marty which is a reply To: "Thomas Merton. Re: Your Prophecy" which was written by Dr. Marty (*The National Catholic Reporter*, 3. 43 (August 30, 1967) 6:1).] *The National Catholic Reporter*, 3.44 (September 6, 1967) 8:1.

C330a "Una Sociedad que Esta Peligrosamente Enferma." *Punto Final* (Chile), XI (Prima quincena de Septiembre de 1967) 14-16.

C331 "Notes on Love." *Frontier*, 3. 10 (Autumn 1967) [211]-214.

C332 [A letter to the editor.] *El Corno Emplumado*, 24 (October, 1967) 155-156.

C332a "The Cultural Cold War: Comments." *The Nation*, CCV (October 9, 1967) 340.

C333 An Interview with Thomas Merton, by Thomas P. McDonnell. *Motive*, 28. 1 (October, 1967) 32-41.

C334 "Teilhard's Gamble/Betting on the Whole Human Species." *The Commonweal*, LXXXVII. 4 (October 27, 1967) 109-111.

C335 "Openness and Cloister" (excerpt: *Contemplation in a World of Action*). *Cistercian Studies*, II. 4 (1967) 312-323.

C336 [A brief comment re] *Le Meditations del Beato Guigo Certosino* (*Guigo the Carthusian*). By M. E. Cristofolini. In *Aevum* 39 (1965) 201-217. *Cistercian Studies*, II. 4 (1967) (*Bulletin of Monastic Spirituality*) (1967) (♯ IV) 61-62.

C337 "Hesychasm." *Diakonia*, 2. 4 (Winter 1967) 380-385.

C338 "Christian Humanism." *Spiritual Life*, 13. 4 (Winter 1967) 219-230.

C339 "La vie solitaire a l'ombre d'un monastere cistercien." *Lettre De Liguge*, 121 (1967) 30-36.

C340 "La vocacion monastica y el ambiente del pensiamento seglar moderno" (excerpt: *Contemplation in a World of Action*) (a Spanish translation of: *Monastic Vocation and Modern Thought*; see C292). *Cuadernos Monasticos*, 4. 5 (1967) 69-91.

C341 " 'Godless Christianity'?" (excerpt: *Faith and Violence*). *Katallagete* (Winter 1967-1968) 15-21.

C342 "The Hot Summer of Sixty-Seven" (excerpt: *Faith and Violence*). *Katallagete* (Winter 1967-1968) 28-34.

C343 "Marcel and Buddha: A Metaphysics of Enlightenment" [an article by] Sally Donnelly, with a Foreword by Thomas Merton. *The Journal of Religious Thought*, XXIV. 1 (1967-1968) 51-57.

C344 "Camus: Journals of the Plague Years." *Sewanee Review*, LXXV. 4 (1967) 717-730.

C345 "Auschwitz: A Family Camp" (excerpt: *Thomas Merton on Peace*). [A review of] *Auschwitz*, by Bernd Naumann, trans. Jean Steinberg, with an introduction by Hannah Arendt. *The Catholic Worker*, XXXIII. 11 (November, 1967) 4:2, 5:1, 8:1.

C346 "War and Vision: The Autobiography of a Crow Indian." [A review of] *Two Leggings: The Making of a Crow Warrior*. By Peter Nabokov. *The Catholic Worker*, XXXIII. 12 (December, 1967) 4:1, 6:5.

C347 "The Time of the End is the Time of no Room" (excerpt: *Raids on the Unspeakable*). *Peace News* (December 22, 1967) 6:1.

C348 "The Cross Fighters/Notes on a Race War." *The Unicorn Journal* (1968) 26-40.

C349 "The Sacred City." *The Catholic Worker*, XXXIV. 1 (January, 1968) 4:1, 5:1, 6:4.

C350 "Meditation in the Woods" (condensed from: *Day of a Stranger*; see C318). *The Catholic Digest*, 32. 3 (January, 1968) 20-24.

C351 "The Spiritual Father in the Desert Tradition" (excerpt: *Contemplation in a World of Action*). *Cistercian Studies*, 3. 1 (1968) 3-23.

C352 "Renouveau De La Formation Monastique." *Collectanea Cisterciensia*, **XXX**. 1 (1968) 211-217.

C353 [Two comments re] *Proposed Canon on Monastic Life*, by L. Meyer, O.S.B., in *The American Benedictine Review* 17 (1966) 354-361; *Monastic Renewal Revisited: Ressourcement and Aggiornamento*, by C. Peifer, O.S.B., in *The American Benedictine Review* 17 (1966) 448-466. *Collectanea Cisterciensia*, **XXX**. 1 (1968) (*Bulletin De Spiritualité Monastique*) (1968) (♯ 1 & 2) 147, 147.

C354 [Three reviews of] *Der monastische Gedanke*. By F. Parpert; *Unamuno y la vida monastica*. By J. Alvarez Arroyo; *The Sin of Sloth: Acedia in Medieval Thought*. By S. Wenzel. *Collectanea Cisterciensia*, **XXX**. 1 (1968) (*Bulletin De Spiritualité Monastique*) (1968) (♯ 1 & 2) 138-140, 140, 173-174.

C355 "Merton: Regains the Old Monastic Charism." [A letter to the editor re Colman McCarthy's article: "Renewal Crisis Hits Trappists" (*The National Catholic Reporter*, 4. 8 (December 13, 1967) 1:2, 5:1).] *The National Catholic Reporter*, 4. 11 (January 11, 1968) 11:1.

C356 "Beyond the Sacred." [A letter re Terry Eagleton's article: "Politics and the Sacred" (December 29, 1967) 402-406.] *The Commonweal*, **LXXXVII**. 15 (January 19, 1968) 479.

C357 "Apertura e vita claustrale" (excerpt: *Contemplation in a World of Action*) (an Italian translation of: *Openness and Cloister*; see C335). *Ora et Labora* (January-March 1968) 11-21.

C357a "Where the Religious Dimension Enters In." *The Center Letter*, 3 (1968) 6.

C358 "Rites for the Extrusion of a Leper." *The Kentucky Review*, II (February, 1968) 26-30.

C358a "Merton's Views on Non-Violence." *World Campus* (February, 1968) 11-12.

C359 "The Vietnam War: An Overwhelming Atrocity" (excerpt: *Faith and Violence*; *Thomas Merton on Peace*). *The Catholic Worker*, XXXIV. 3 (March, 1968) 1:2, 6:1, 7:3.

C359a "Letter to the Editor on Vietnam." *U. S. Catholic*, XXXIII (March, 1968) 44.

C360 "The Sacred City" (condensed from *The Catholic Worker*; see C349). *The Center Magazine*, I. 3 (March, 1968) 73-77.

C360a "A Catch of Anti-Letters." (Correspondence between Robert Lax and Thomas Merton.) *Voyages*, II (Winter-Spring 1968) 44-56.

C361 "The Spiritual Father in the Desert Tradition" (excerpt: *Contemplation in a World of Action*). *Monastic Studies*, 5 (Easter 1968) 87-111.

C362 "Contemplation in a World of Action" (excerpt: *Contemplation in a World of Action*). *Bloominewman* (Newsletter of the Newman Club of the University of Louisville), II (April, 1968) 1-5.

C362a "The Way of Chuang Tzu" (excerpt: *The Way of Chuang Tzu*). *The Mountain Path*, V (April, 1968) 102-105.

C363 "The Historical Consciousness." *The Contemplative Review*, I (May, 1968) 203.

C364 "Who Is Nat Turner?" [A review of] *The Confessions of Nat Turner*. By William Styron. *Katallagete* (Spring 1968) 20-23.

C364a "My Campaign Platform for non-Abbot and permanent keeper of the Present Doghouse." *Unicorn Journal*, I (Spring 1968) 95-96.

C364b "The Spiritual Father in the Desert Tradition" (excerpt: *Contemplation in a World of Action*). *Newsletter-Review* (The R. M. Bucke Memorial Society, Montreal), III (Spring 1968) 7-21.

C365 "The Monk Today" (excerpt: *Contemplation in a World of Action*). *Latitudes*, II. 1 (Spring 1968) 10-14.

C366 "Dialogue and Renewal in the Contemplative Life" (excerpt: *Contemplation in a World of Action*). *Spiritual Life*, 14. 1 (Spring 1968) 41-52.

C367 "Ecumenism and Monastic Renewal" (excerpt: *Contemplation in a World of Action*). *Journal of Ecumenical Studies*, 5. 2 (Spring 1968) 268-283.

C368 "The Wild Places." *The Catholic Worker*, XXXIV. 5 (June, 1968) 4:1, 6:1.

C369 " 'baptism in the forest': wisdom and initiation in william faulkner" (excerpt: *Introductory Essay*; see B58). *The Catholic World*, 207. 1239 (June, 1968) 124-130.

C369a "The Study of Zen" (excerpt: *Zen and the Birds of Appetite*). *Cimarron Review*, 4 (June, 1968) 38-49.

C370 "The Wild Places" (condensed from *The Catholic Worker*; see C368). *The Center Magazine*, I. 5 (July, 1968) 40-44.

C371 "The Secular Saint." [A letter re Michael Novak's article: "The Secular Saint" (May, 1968) 50-59.] *The Center Magazine*, I. 5 (July, 1968) 93-94.

C371a "War and Vision." [A review of] *Two Leggings: The Maturing of a Crow Warrior*. By Peter Nabokov. *Theoria to Theory*, II (July, 1968) 336.

C372 "Notes on the New Church at Gethsemani." *Liturgical Arts*, 36. 4 (August, 1968) 100-101.

C373 "Rites for the Extrusion of a Leper" (condensed from *The Kentucky Review*; see C358). *Peace News* (August 30, 1968) 6:1.

C373a "Correspondence" [Note on Joyce's Ulysses]. *Sewanee Review*, LXXVI. 4 (1968) [694].

C374 "Hesychasm." [A review of] "Hesychasme et priere" (*Coll. Orientalia Christiana Analecta* 176). By I. Hausherr, S.J. *Cistercian Studies*, III. 2 (1968) (*Bulletin of Monastic Spirituality*) (1968) (#I) 84-88.

C375 Renewal in Monastic Education (excerpt: *Contemplation in a World of Action*). *Cistercian Studies*, III. 3 (1968) 247-252.

C376 [A summary of] "Monasterium-Carcer (Prison)," by G. Penco, in *Studia Monastica* 8 (1966) 133-143. *Cistercian Studies*, III. 3 (1968) (*Bulletin of Monastic Spirituality*) (1968) (# III) 110.

C377 "Peace and Revolution: A Footnote from Ulysses" (excerpt: *Thomas Merton on Peace*). *Peace*, III (1968) 5-10.

C378 "Letter to a Bishop" (August, 1968). *Peace*, III (1968) 11-12.

C379 "Nonviolence Does Not, Cannot Mean Passivity." *Ave Maria*, 108. 8 (September 7, 1968) 9-10.

C380 "Three Saviors in Camus." *Thought*, XLIII. 168 (September, 1968) [5]-23.

C381 Excerpts from a Letter from Father Thomas Merton. *The Center Letter*, III (1968) 7; IV (1968) 7.

C382 "The Conquest of France: Speech and Testimonals, 1941." *Monks Pond*, 3 (Fall 1968) 71-78.

C383 "Solitude" (excerpt: *Contemplation in a World of Action*). *Spiritual Life*, 14. 3 (Fall 1968) 171-178.

C383a "The Stranger: Poverty of an Anti-Hero." *Unicorn Journal*, I (Fall 1968) 10-19.

C384 "Final Integration Toward a 'Monastic Therapy'" (excerpt: *Contemplation in a World of Action*). *Monastic Studies*, 6 (1968) 87-99.

C385 "Blake and the New Theology." *Sewanee Review*, LXXVI. 4 (1968) 673-682.

C385a Reply by Thomas Merton to Comment on his Review of *Two Leggings: The Maturing of a Crow Indian* (see C371a). *Theoria to Theory*, III (October, 1968) 90-91.

C385b "Two Comments: Sensitivity Training; The Avant-Garde in the Arts." *Forum*, I (October, 1968) 30-33.

C386 [A brief comment on the Racial Crisis.] (Excerpt: *Faith and Violence*.) The Catholic Worker, XXXIV. 9 (November, 1968) 1:1.

C387 "Asian Letter" (to his friends; from New Delhi, India, written on November 9, 1968; a postcard from Singapore which he wrote on December 5, 1968). *Cistercian Studies*, III. 4 (1968) 272-276, 276.

C388 Thomas Merton/1915-1968/Excerpts from/ Commonweal: "Contemplative Life" (from *Poetry and the Contemplative Life*; see A5, B3, C14); "Christmas" (from *A Christmas Devotion*; see C19); "Art" (from *Reality, Art, and Prayer*; see C84); "Nuclear War" (from *Nuclear War and Christian Responsibility*; see C168); "The World" (from *Is the World a Problem?*; see C279). *The Commonweal*, LXXXIX. 13 (December 27, 1968) 435, 435-436, 436, 437, 437.

C389 [Three comments re] *Los Monasterios de monjas en Galicia (Galician nuns)*, by G. Martinez, in *Yermo* 4 (1966) 51-78; *Les chrétientés celtiques (Celtic monasticism)*, by O. Loyer; *The Dream of the Rood and Anglo-Saxon Monasticism*, by J. Fleming, in *Traditio* 22 (1966) 43-72. *Cistercian Studies*, III. 4 (1968) (*Bulletin of Monastic Spirituality*) (1968) (♯ III) 119, 119, 120.

C390 [Six comments re] *Saint Bruno, le premier des ermites de Chartreuse*, by A. Ravier, S.J.; *Los monasterios de Benedictinos de Galicia*, by M. Arias, in *Studia Monastica* 8 (1966) 35-69; *The Grandmontines/A Forgotten Order*, by D. Seward, in *The Downside Review* 83 (1965) 249-264; *Isaac De L'Etoile, Sermons, t. I.* Texte et introduction critiques par Anselme Hoste, O.S.B., introduction, traduction et notes par Gaston Salet, S.J. (*Coll. Sources Chretiennes* 130, *Serie des textes monastiques d'Occident* 20); *Gertrude D'Helfta (Saint Gertrude) Oeuvres spirituelles, t. I. Les exercices.* Texte Latin, introduction, traduction et notes par Jacques Hourlier et Albert Schmitt.

(*Coll. Sources Chretiennes* 127, *Serie des textes monastiques d'Occident* 19); *L'érémitisme à la Catalunya nova (Eremitism)*, by E. Fort Cogul, in Studia Monastica 7 (1965) 63-126. *Cistercian Studies*, III. 4 (1968) (*Bulletin of Monastic Spirituality*) (1968) (♯ IV) 126-127, 127, 127-128, 139, 141-142, 144.

C391 [Three comments re] *Mallorca eremitica, por un Ermitano* (*Eremitism in Mallorca*), Imp. *Sagrados Corazones; Monasterios y monjes en los (Diarios de Jovellanos*) (*Don Gaspar Melchor de Jovellanos*), by I. M. Gomez, in *Yermo* 4 (1966) 107-213; Un manual de ermitanos (A handbook for hermits), by G. M. Colombas, in *Yermo* 3 (1965) 317-333. *Cistercian Studies*, III. 4 (1968) (*Bulletin of Monastic Spirituality*) (1968) (♯ V) 148, 151, 154.

C392 [A letter and an article:] *Lettera dall'Asia* (see C387); *Note Sul Futuro Del Monachesimo* (excerpt: *Action in a World of Contemplation*). *L'Osservatore Romano* (Italian), 7. 32.985 (10 Gennaio 1969) 3, 3.

C393 "Merton: View of Monasticism. Seeking God Through Total Love Is Goal." [Extemporaneous talk delivered at Spiritual Summit Conference in Calcutta, October 22-26, 1968.] *The Washington Post* (January 18, 1969) C9:1.

C394 [Two letters] "On the Future of Monasticism," written at Gethsemani 23 June 1968; "Buddhist Monasticism and Meditation," written at New Delhi 11 November 1968. *L'Osservatore Romano* (English), 4. 43 (January 23, 1969) 5, 10.

C395 "As Man to Man." *Cistercian Studies*, IV. 1 (1969) 90-94.

C396 "Notes on the Future of Monasticism" (excerpt: *Action in a World of Contemplation*) (reprinted from *L'Osservatore Romano*) (see C392) and revised for *Monastic Exchange*, 1 (1969) 9-13.

C397 "Lettre D'Asie" (see C387, C392). *Collectanea Cisterciensia*, 31. 1 (1969) 14-18.

C398 "Dieu n'est pas un probleme." *Collectanea Cisterciensia*, 31. 1 (1969) 19-23.

C398a "The Monk as Marginal Man." *The Center Magazine* (1969) 32.

C399 "Ouverture et cloture" (excerpt: *Contemplation in a World of Action*) (a French translation of: Openness and Cloister; see C335). *Collectanea Cisterciensia*, 31. 1 (1969) 24-35.

C399a "A New Christian Consciousness." *Theoria to Theory*, III (January, 1969) 5-8.

C399b "Amor y necesidad." *Sur*, 316-317 (January-April 1969) [38]-46.

C399c "Contemplation and Dialogue between Religions." *Sobornost*, V (Winter-Spring 1969) 562-570.

C399d "Todas las tardes Atlas vigila" (excerpt: *Raids on the Unspeakable*). *Sur*, 316-317 (January-April 1969) [47]-52.

C400 "An Anti-Poem, Plessy vs. Ferguson: Theme and Variations" (see B69). *The Commonweal*, LXXXIX. 8 (February 7, 1969) 592-593.

C401 "Creative Silence." *The Baptist Student*, XLVIII (February, 1969) 18-22.

C402 "Terror and the Absurd: Violence and Nonviolence in Albert Camus." *Motive*, XXIX. 5 (February, 1969) 5-15.

C403 "The Burning of Papers/The Human Conscience/And the Peace Movement" (first published in *Ave Maria*; see C379). *Fellowship*, 35. 3 (March, 1969) 7-8.

C404 [A letter to the editor.] *Spiritual Life*, 15. 1 (Spring 1969) 3.

C405 "Openness and Cloister" (excerpt: *Contemplation in a World of Action*). *Spiritual Life*, 15. 1 (Spring 1969) 26-36.

C406 [The Japanese Tea Ceremony.] *Good Work*, XXXII. 2 (Spring 1969) 6.

C407 "The Street is for Celebration." *The Mediator*, XX (Summer 1969) 2-4.

C407a Letter to Mr. T. L. Dickson, Manager of the Bookstore. *The University of Delaware Religious Book Guide* (July-August 1970) 10.

C408 [Four comments re] "Aphorisms for a Contemplative," by J. Carmody, S.J., in *The American Benedictine Review* 17 (1966) 519-522; "Community: A Monastic Witness," by Sister Agnes Shaw, O.S.B., in *The American Benedictine Review* 17 (1966) 409-435; *Der monastische Gedanke (Protestant monasticism)*, by F. Parpert; "Unamuno y la vida monastica," by J. Alvarez Arroyo, in *Yermo* 4 (1966) 1-50. *Cistercian Studies*, IV. 2 (1969) (*Bulletin of Monastic Spirituality*) (1969) (♯ I) 158, 159-160, 166-167, 167-168.

C409 "The Solitary Life." *Cistercian Studies*, IV. 3 (1969) 213-217.

C410 [A comment re] "Monastic Renewal Revisited: Ressourcement and Aggiornamento," by C. Peifer, O.S.B., in *The American Benedictine Review* 17 (1966) 448-466. *Cistercian Studies*, IV. 3 (1969) (*Bulletin of Monastic Spirituality*) (1969) (♯ I) 173.

C411 "Canon law." [A comment re] "Proposed Canon on Monastic Life," by L. Meyer, O.S.B., in *The American Benedictine Review* 17 (1966) 354-361. *Cistercian Studies*, IV. 3 (1969) (*Bulletin of Monastic Spirituality*) (1969) (♯ I) 173-174.

C412 "The concept of acedia." [A review of] "The Sin of Sloth: Acedia in Medieval Thought and Literature," by S. Wenzel. *Cistercian Studies*, IV. 3 (1969) (*Bulletin of Monastic Spirituality*) (1969) (♯ II) 201.

C413 "Writing as Temperature." *Sewanee Review*, LXXVII. 3 (1969) 535-542.

C414 "News of the Joyce Industry." *Sewanee Review*, LXXVII. 3 (1969) 543-554.

C415 "A Letter from Thomas Merton." *Sewanee Review*, LXXVII. 3 (1969) 555-556.

C416 "Meditation." *L'Osservatore Romano*, 40. 79 (October 2, 1969) 6.

C417 [Two comments re] "Relevancy of the Rule Today," by Sister M. W. McPherson, O.S.B., in *The American Benedictine Review* 17 (1966) 41-51; "Civil Rights of the Monk in Roman and Canon Law/The Monk as 'Servus'

(The monk as a slave)," by P. M. Blecker, O.S.B., in
The American Benedictine Review 17 (1966) 185-198.
Cistercian Studies, IV. 4 (1969) (*Bulletin of Monastic
Spirituality*) (1969) (♯ III) 209, 213.

C418 "Is the 'Contemplative Life' Finished?" (excerpt:
Contemplation in a World of Action). *Monastic Studies*, 7
(Michaelmas 1969) 11-62.

C419 "Monachesimo del futuro: quale?" *Vita Monastica*,
XXIII. 96 (1969) 3-15.

C420 "The Contemplative and the Atheist" (excerpt:
Contemplation in a World of Action). *Schema* XIII, 1.
1 (January, 1970) 11-18.

C421 "Renewal and Discipline in the Monastic Life" (excerpt:
Contemplation in a World of Action). *Cistercian Studies*,
5. 1 (1970) 3-18.

C422 "A Conference on Prayer." *Sisters Today*, 41. 8
(April, 1970) 449-456.

C423 "A Life Free from Care." *Cistercian Studies*, 5. 3
(1970) 217-226.

C424 "La vida solitaria al amparo de un monasterio
cisterciense" (a Spanish translation of: "La vie solitaire
a l'ombre d'un monastere cistercien"; see C339).
Cistercium 22 (1970) 205-213.

C425 "This is God's Work." *Sisters Today*, 42. 1 (August,
1970) 1-7.

C426 "The Life that Unifies." *Sisters Today*, 42. 2 (October,
1970) 65-73.

C427 "Prayer, Personalism, and the Spirit." *Sisters Today*, 42. 3 (November, 1970) 129-136.

C428 "Opening the Bible?" (excerpt: *Opening the Bible*). *The Bible Today*, L (November, 1970) 104-113.

C429 "Building Community on God's Love." *Sisters Today*, 42. 4 (December, 1970) 185-193.

C430 "Community, Politics, and Contemplation." *Sisters Today*, 42. 5 (January, 1971) 241-246.

C431 "Prayer, Tradition, and Experience." *Sisters Today*, 42. 6 (February, 1971) 285-293.

C432 "Contemplation in a World of Action." *Sisters Today*, 42. 7 (March, 1971) 345-351.

C433 "Prayer and Conscience." *Sisters Today*, 42. 8 (April, 1971) 409-418.

C434 "Cistercians and Study." *Cistercian Studies*, 6. 2 (1971) 180-183.

C435 "The Face: Tertullian and St. Cyprian on Virgins." *Cistercian Studies*, 6. 4 (1971) 334-342.

C436 "Lactantius." *Cistercian Studies*, 7. 4 (1972) 243-255.

C437 "Guerric of Igny's Easter Sermons." *Cistercian Studies*, 7. 1 (1972) [85]-95.

C438 "To Live is to Love" (see B77). *United States Catholic and Jubilee*, 37. 3 (March, 1972) 19-23.

C439 "Time and Unburdening and the Recollection of the Lamb: The Easter Service in Faulkner's *The Sound and the Fury*." (Article has An Introductory Note by Brother Patrick Hart.) *Katallagete*, 4. 4 (Summer 1973) 7-15.

C440 "The Eastward Flight/October 15" [1968]; "Bangkok/
December 7" [1968]; "The Last Entry/December 8"
[1968] (excerpt: *The Asian Journal of Thomas Merton*).
The Critic, XXXI. 6 (July-August 1973) 44-45,
45-46, 46-47.

C441 "The Asian Journal of Thomas Merton" (excerpt:
The Asian Journal of Thomas Merton). *Intellectual
Digest*, IV. 3 (November, 1973) 57-64.

C442 "Is the World a Problem?" (excerpt: *Contemplation
in a World of Action*) (see C279, C388). *The
Commonweal*, XCIX. 7 (November 16, 1973) 177-179.

C443 [A brief quotation] (excerpt: *Raids on the Unspeakable*). *The Catholic Worker*, XXXIX. 9 (December,
1973) 2:1.

D. Translations by Thomas Merton

D1 *The Kingdom of Jesus* (1946)
THE LIFE AND THE KINGDOM / OF JESUS / IN
CHRISTIAN SOULS / A TREATISE ON CHRISTIAN
PERFECTION / FOR USE BY CLERGY OR LAITY /
BY / SAINT JOHN EUDES / Translated from the French
by / A Trappist Father [Thomas Merton] in / The
Abbey of Our Lady of Gethsemani / With an Introduction
by / THE RIGHT REVEREND / MONSIGNOR
[now Bishop] FULTON J. SHEEN / [publisher's device] /
NEW YORK / P. J. KENEDY & SONS
   3 leaves, v-xxxv, 1 leaf, 3-348 pp. 21 x 14½ cm. $3.00.
Navy blue cloth with device imprinted in gold on front
cover; lettered in gold on spine. Bright blue dust-wrapper,
with medallion of Saint John Eudes, printed in black
on front cover and spine.
   [Published: April 10, 1946.]

D2 *The Soul of the Apostolate* (1946)
 a *Cloth edition*:
The Soul / of the / Apostolate / By / Dom Jean-Baptiste
Chautard, O.C.S.O. / (Abbot of Notre Dame de
Sept-Fons) / 55TH THOUSAND / in U. S. A. / Complete
new translation / by / A Monk [Thomas Merton]
of Our Lady of Gethsemani
   2 leaves, [v]-xxii, 1 leaf, [1]-290 pp., 1 leaf, 2 blank

leaves. 18 x 12 cm. $3.00. Black leather lettered in gold on front cover and downward on spine. No dust-wrapper. Edges stained red.

[Published: September 16, 1946, by the Monks of Our Lady of Gethsemani, Trappist, Kentucky.]

b *Paper-back edition*:

THE SOUL OF / THE APOSTOLATE / BY / Dom Jean-Baptiste Chautard, O.C.S.O. / TRANSLATED, AND WITH AN INTRODUCTION / By THOMAS MERTON / [publisher's symbol] / IMAGE BOOKS / A Division of Doubleday & Company, Inc. / Garden City, New York

270 pp., 5 leaves. 18¼ x 10½ cm. $0.85. Pale blue paper, with Christian design, printed in dark green and black on front cover and downward on spine.

On verso of title-page: Image Books Edition published September, 1961 / 1st printing _ _ _ _ _ _ _ _ _ _ _ _ August, 1961

D3 *The Spirit of Simplicity* (1948)

The Cistercian Library. No. 3. / The / Spirit of Simplicity / Characteristic of the Cistercian Order / An Official Report, / demanded and approved by the / GENERAL CHAPTER / Together with Texts from / ST. BERNARD OF CLAIRVAUX / on Interior Simplicity / Translation and Commentary by / A Cistercian Monk [Thomas Merton] of Our Lady of Gethsemani / TRAPPIST, KENTUCKY / 1948

4 leaves, ii-[vii], [1]-139 pp., 1 blank leaf. 18½ x 12 cm. $1.75. Black cloth lettered in gold on front cover and downward on spine. No dust-wrapper.

Illustrated with 12 sepia photographs of ancient and modern Cistercian architecture which were taken by Jahan and Sauvageot, and a detailed sketch, with explanatory notes, of a typical Cistercian abbey in the 12th century.

[Published: April 23, 1948, by the Monks of Our Lady
of Gethsemani, Trappist, Kentucky.]

D4 *The Wisdom of the Desert* (1961)
 a *Cloth edition*:
 THE WISDOM / OF THE DESERT / Sayings from the
 Desert Fathers / of the Fourth Century / TRANSLATED /
 BY THOMAS MERTON / A NEW DIRECTIONS
 BOOK
  4 leaves, ix, [1-2]-3-81 pp., 2 blank leaves. 22 x 14½ cm.
 $3.50. Oyster-white linen cloth lettered downward on
 spine in brown; brown end-papers. Dark brown
 dust-wrapper printed in white, black and yellow on front
 cover and downward on spine.
 [Published: April 26, 1961.]

 b *Paper-back edition*:
 THE WISDOM / OF THE DESERT / Sayings from the
 Desert Fathers / of the Fourth Century / TRANSLATED /
 BY THOMAS MERTON / A NEW DIRECTIONS
 BOOK
  4 leaves, ix, [1-2]-3-81 pp., 1 leaf. 20½ x 13½ cm.
 $1.50. Light grey paper printed in black on front cover
 and downward on spine. Cover photograph by Roloff Beny.
 [Published: November, 1969.]

D5 *Clement of Alexandria* (1963)
 [Title lettered in green] Clement of Alexandria / Selections
 from / THE PROTREPTIKOS / AN ESSAY / AND
 TRANSLATION / BY / THOMAS MERTON / NEW
 DIRECTIONS
  1 blank leaf, 3 leaves, 1-27 pp., 1 leaf, 1 blank leaf.
 18½ x 12½ cm. $1.50. Pebbled-grey paper printed in
 green on front cover and upward on spine.

Colophon (p. [29]) : SET IN DANTE TYPE AND
PRINTED / AT THE STAMPERIA VALDONEGA /
VERONA · MCMLXII
[Published: February 7, 1963.]

D6 *The Solitary Life* (1963)
THE / [second and third word of title lettered in red]
SOLITARY LIFE / A LETTER OF / GUIGO /
INTRODUCED AND / TRANSLATED FROM THE
LATIN BY / THOMAS MERTON / * * * /
WORCESTER / 1963
2 leaves, 1-11 pp. 14½ x 10½ cm. (No Price.)
Green and black paper, in a mosaic design, printed in
gold on front cover.
Colophon (p. [12]) : Copyright / Abbey of
Gethsemani / & printed in England at the / Stanbrook
Abbey Press, Worcester / [publisher's symbol] / Setting
in Spectrum with Romulus Open initials / Blocking &
binding by George Percival / Cover paper by Birgitta
Cramer / December 1963
[Published: December, 1963.]

D7 *A Prayer of Cassiodorus* (1967)
[On verso of leaf 1 is the following:] PREFACE &
TRANSLATION BY / THOMAS MERTON / FROM
THE TREATISE / DE ANIMA / STANBROOK
ABBEY PRESS 1967 [Title-page lettered in red]
A PRAYER / OF / CASSIODORUS
4 blank leaves, 3 leaves, 1-15 pp., 1 leaf, 4 blank leaves.
26 x 13½ cm. (No Price.) Off-white cloth, with mosaic
design in beige, white, blue and brown on front and
back cover. No dust-wrapper.
Colophon (p. [17]) : Text of the Prayer / handset in 12
point *Monotype Spectrum* / Preface machine-set in

10 point / by Westype Ltd, Bristol / Re-justified by hand
and / printed in England at the / Stanbrook Abbey Press,
Worcester / on *August Badger* handmade paper / from
Hayle Mill, Maidstone / Bound by George Percival,
Leicester / Cover paper marbled by / Douglass Cockerell
& Son, Cambridge
     On recto of leaf 1: [Copyright] Abbey of Gethsemani /
March 1967
     [Published: March, 1967.]

E. Miscellanea, Recordings, Privately Printed Material

E1 *The Waters of Silence* (1950)
   First English de Luxe edition:
   THE WATERS / OF SILENCE / [English version of
   The Waters of Siloe; see A11.] / by / THOMAS
   MERTON / With a Foreword by / Evelyn Waugh /
   [device] / THEODORE BRUN LIMITED, LONDON /
   98, Great Russel Street, W.C.1
   6 leaves, 3-299 pp. 22½ x 15½ cm. 32s. Black leather
   with design by George Motte imprinted in gold on front
   cover; lettered in gold on spine; photographed end-papers
   by Yvonne Sauvageot. Top edges stained gold.
   No dust-wrapper.
   36 photographs.
   On verso of title-page: This Limited de Luxe Edition
   is published / by special arrangement with Messrs.
   Hollis & / Carter, Ltd., London, and appears simultane- /
   ously with their first edition. One hundred / and twenty
   copies have been printed for sale. In / addition, five copies,
   numbered I to V, have / been struck off as presentation
   and reference / copies. / No. 86 [written in ink]
   [Published: July 21, 1950.]
   This version, as in the Hollis and Carter issue, has
   deletions of sections and transpositions of chapters, e.g.,
   the "Prologue" and a "Note on the Function of a
   Contemplative Order" which comprise the beginning

in the American edition are eliminated. The title heading
of Chapter I in the two English and American editions
is similar, but Chapter II of the English editions reads:
"Cistercian Life in the Twelfth Century," which in the
American edition is Chapter XII. In the latter edition,
Chapter II reads: "De Rance and La Trappe," which
in the English edition becomes Chapter III. From here on
the original sequence of chapter headings follows;
however, Chapter XIII of the American edition which reads:
"The Cistercian Character and Sanctity," has been entirely
omitted in the English editions. Thus Chapter XIII in
the latter editions reads: "Paradisus Claustralis," which
in the American edition is Chapter XIV. This is followed
by an Appendix, e.g., "The Daily Life of a Cistercian
in our Time" (in the American edition it was appended
after the "Table of Contents"), a "Bibliography"
and an "Index"; the "Glossary of Some Monastic Terms"
is not included.

E2 *Selected Poems of Thomas Merton* (1950)
  First English edition:
  SELECTED / POEMS / BY / THOMAS MERTON /
  WITH A FOREWORD BY / ROBERT SPEAIGHT /
  LONDON / HOLLIS & CARTER / 1950
    2 leaves, v-xii, 1 leaf, 3-113 pp., 1 blank leaf. $22\frac{1}{2}$ x 15
  cm. 12 / 6. Sand colored cloth lettered upward in gold
  on green rectangle on spine. Top edges stained green.
  Chartreuse dust-wrapper printed in maroon with design.
    [Published: November 29, 1950.]
    Contents: Excerpts from Merton's four books of poetry: 14
  from THIRTY POEMS; 25 from A MAN IN THE DIVIDED
  SEA; 15 from FIGURES FOR AN APOCALYPSE; 11 from THE
  TEARS OF THE BLIND LIONS. Included in this collection is
  a hitherto unpublished poem: SPORTS WITHOUT BLOOD / A
  Letter to [the late] Dylan Thomas. (This has since appeared in
  America; see A25, F55).

E3 *Marthe, Marie et Lazare* (1956)
First French paper-back edition:
PRESENCE CHRETIENNE / [horizontal line across title-page] / Thomas Merton / MARTHE, / MARIE / et / LAZARE / DESCLEE DE BROUWER
145 pp., 1 leaf. 19 x 12 cm. (No Price.) Pale green paper printed in black and red on front cover and upward on spine in red.
On verso of title-page: . . . traduit de l'anglais par Juliette Charles-Du Bos.
[Published: December, 1956.]
Numerous universities and libraries were visited but I could not track down an American version of this book; nor was I able to pinpoint, in the many indexes consulted, a listing of articles that later became the nucleus of Marthe, Marie et Lazare.

E4 *La Montée vers la Lumiere* (1958)
First French de Luxe revised edition:
THOMAS MERTON / LA MONTÉE / VERS LA / LUMIERE / (THE ASCENT TO TRUTH) / Traduit de l'americain / par / MARIE TADIE / EDITIONS ALBIN MICHEL / 22, rue Huyghens / PARIS
2 blank leaves, 4 leaves, 9-233 pp., 2 leaves, 1 blank leaf. 20½ x 13 cm. (No Price.) Black simulated leather with Christian symbol imprinted in gold on front cover and lettered across on spine in gold. No dust-wrapper.
On verso of title-page: Il a été tire de cet ouvrage: / 300 exemplaires sur alfama du Marais, / dont 300 numerotes de 1 a 300, / et 10 hors commerce numerotes / de I a X. EXEMPLAIRE H. C. Nº 11 [written in ink]
[Published: March, 1958.]
In revising the French edition of "Ascent", Merton decided to reshape and shorten the Prologue, cut out the Biographical Notes and Sources, as well as Chapters 1, 2, and 4 which are in the American version. The edited work begins with Chapters 1 to 16 which in the American edition are Chapters 3, 5 and on to 19.

E5 *Salve Regina* (1960)

First edition: [Sheet Music]

The Trappist Cistercian / [reads downward] / Salve /
Regina / accompaniment / musical and historical notes /
a meditation on the text / by Thomas Merton

[8] pp. 30½ x 23½ cm. (No Price.) Royal blue paper,
with symbolic design, printed in white on front cover.

[Published by the Abbey of Gethsemani (January,
1960).]

E6 *Victor Hammer* (1965)

First edition:

VICTOR HAMMER / A RETROSPECTIVE EXHIBI-
TION / APRIL 4-25, 1965 / NORTH CAROLINA
MUSEUM OF ART, RALEIGH

91 pp. 25½ x 19 cm. (No Price.) Off-white paper printed
in black on front cover and downward on spine. Cover:
Detail from Mnemosyne and Her Daughters, The Muses /
Tempera and gold leaf on panel; 39¼" x 24¼"
(overall) / Catalog Number 23

The work contains a Foreword by Merton (pp. 4-6)
and a painting: THOMAS MERTON (1962) / Tempera
on panel; 13⅜" x 12" / Catalog Number 26), p. 6.

[No publication date.]

E7 *Redeeming the Time* (1966)

REDEEMING / THE TIME / THOMAS MERTON /
LONDON / BURNS & OATES

187 pp., 2 blank leaves. 20 x 13 cm. 12s 6d. White paper
printed in black and red on front and back cover and
downward on spine.

On verso of title-page: This Burns & Oates edition
first published in 1966

Contents: The Church And The "Godless World"—The
"World"—"Godless Christianity"?—God and the World— The
Protest of Vitalism—Christian Humanism in the Nuclear Era—
The Road Ahead

The last two essays in *Redeeming the Time: The
Christian in the Diaspora* (93-119), and *The Christian in
World Crisis* (120-187) were first published in America
by Farrar, Straus and Giroux in 1964 under the title:
Seeds of Destruction (see table of contents, A42).

E8 *Vietnam and the American Conscience* (1966)
    A Program:
    Town / Hall / 123 West 43d Street, New York, N.Y. /
    New York University
    [4] pp. 25 x 17½ cm. White paper printed in black
    on front cover. The program which was issued at a
    rally held at Town Hall on June 9, 1966, re the war in
    Vietnam and the American conscience was highlighted by
    an article of Merton's: "NHAT HANH IS MY
    BROTHER" (p. 2) (excerpt: Faith and Violence;
    Thomas Merton on Peace).
    [Published: June 2, 1966.]

RECORDINGS

E9 The Harvard Vocarium Records: 1950 (78 RPM, 1 12"
    record, ♯L 1018; 2 sides). A reading of his selected verse
    by Robert Speaight. Side 1: "The Trappist Cemetery"
    (from *A Man in the Divided Sea*); side 2: Band 1:
    "In the Rain and the Sun"; Band 2: "A Psalm" (from
    The Tears of the Blind Lions).

E10 Columbia Masterworks: April 2, 1951 (LP, 33 1/3 RPM,
    1 12" record, ♯ML 54394; 2 sides) [also supplied in 78

RPM, 4 12″ records, ♯MM 1021]. Side 1: "Laudate
Dominum:" Gregorian Chant by the Trappist Monks
of the Abbey of Gethsemani, Kentucky; side 2: "Laudes
Vespertinae: Hymns in Honor of the Blessed Virgin
Mary"; with program notes by Thomas Merton.

When this record was issued, it was erroneously believed (and
still is) that the running commentary was the voice of Thomas
Merton; actually, the voice used is that of another member of the
Gethsemani community.

Laudate Dominum: Band 1: "Exsurge" (Introit for
Septuagesima)—Band 2: "Lutum Fecit" (Communion,
Antiphon for the Mass of Wed. after IV Lent)—
Band 3: "Quinque Prudentes" (From Common Mass of
Virgins)—Band 4: "Puer" (Introit of the Principal
Mass of Christmas)—Band 5: "Vox in Rama" (Communion
Antiphon of Holy Innocents)—Band 6: "Videns
Dominus" (Communion of Mass for the Sat. after IV
Lent)—Band 7: "Collegerunt" (Responsory from
the Palm Sun. Procession)—Band 8: "Nemo Te"
(Communion of the Mass for Sat. after III Lent)—Band
9: "Mane Nobiscum" (Antiphon from the Corpus Christi
Office)—Band 10: "Dirigatur" (Gradual of Mass for
Tue. after I Lent)—Band 11: "Beatus Bernardus"
(Cistercian Responsory for the Feast of St. Bernard)
Laudes Vespertinae: Band 1: "Ave Maria"—Band 2:
"Magnificat"—Band 3: "Ego Dormio"—Band 4: "Salve
Mater Misericordiae"—Band 5: "Toto Pulchra Es"—
Band 6: "Rosa Vernans"—Band 7: "Salve Regina" (Hymn
to the Blessed Virgin Mary sung ["after Compline"])

"After Compline," according to a note from Thomas Merton, is
more exact and to the point than the actual wording on the
slip-case: ". . . sung at the conclusion of the Divine Office."

E11 *The Merton Tapes*. Electronic Paperbacks issued 12 hour-
long cassettes taken from informal novice conferences

taped by Thomas Merton at the Abbey of Gethsemani
during the years immediately preceding his death. The
cassettes came out in November 1972 and sell for $7.95
each; the complete set at $85.00. Titles and number follow:

    TM-1   "Life and Prayer: The Desert Source"
    TM-2   "Life and Prayer: Journey in Christ"
    TM-3   "Life and Prayer: The Jesus Prayer"
    TM-4   "Life and Contemplation"
    TM-5   "Life and the Holy Spirit"
    TM-6   "Life and God's Love"
    TM-7   "Life and Truth"
    TM-8   "Life and Solitude"
    TM-9   "Life and Prophecy"
    TM-10 "Life and Work"
    TM-11 "Life and Community"
    TM-12 "Life and Celebration"

PRIVATELY PRINTED MATERIAL

(The items described in this section do not form a part of my
library. The bibliographical information was supplied from a
catalog which details, in part, the Collection of Victor Hammer
Imprints.)

E12 [First private printing of] *The Unquiet Conscience*,
    by Piero Bargellini; trans. Thomas Merton. A four-page
    booklet. "Best wishes from Carolyn and Victor Hammer"—
    card laid in. Lexington, Kentucky, Carolyn and Victor
    Hammer (no month; 1958).

E13 [First private printing of] "What Ought I To Do?
    Sayings of the Desert Fathers" (excerpt: *The Wisdom
    of the Desert*; excerpted in Harper's Bazaar; see C150).
    "These sayings of the Fathers (Verba Seniorum) are
    drawn from the classical collection that goes by that name."

Translated from Migne's Latin Patrology by Thomas
Merton. Lexington: Stamperia del Santuccio, 1959.
(Notes: printed in red and black from American Uncial
type; fifty copies numbered at the press; autographed copy.)

E14 [First private printing of] *The Solitary Life*, by
Thomas Merton. "If You Seek A Heavenly Light,"
poem, on book jacket (excerpt: *Emblems of a Season of
Fury*; p. 38). Lexington: Stamperia del Santuccio, 1960.
(Notes: printed in red and black from American Uncial
type; title-page printed from Andromaque, a cursive
uncial, here used for the first time; sixty copies numbered
at the press; autographed copy.)

E15 [First private printing of] *The Ox Mountain Parable of
Meng Tzu* (see C154), [by Thomas Merton.] Lexington:
Stamperia del Santuccio, 1960. (Notes: printed in black,
red, blue from American Uncial type; initial letters in
28-pt; one-hundred copies numbered at the press.)

E16 [First private printing of] "Hagia Sophia" (excerpt:
Emblems of a Season of Fury; pp. 61-69; article was also
published in *Ramparts*; see C194), by Thomas Merton.
Lexington: Stamperia del Santuccio, 1962. (Notes:
printed in red and black from American Uncial type;
title-page printed from Andromaque type; 69 copies
numbered at the press; autographed copy.)

E17 [First private printing of] *Boris Pasternak / Thomas
Merton / Six Letters*. Foreword [by] Naomi Burton Stone /
Introduction [by] Lydia Pasternak Slater [sister of the
author of Doctor Zhivago]. Lexington: University of
Kentucky (The King Library Press), 1973. (Notes:
Composition, press work, and binding by Gray Zeitz /

Mabel B. DuPriest, Travis DuPriest, Margaret A. /
Williams, Ida Nieves-Collazo, Christopher Meatyard /
(apprentices to Carolyn Hammer at the King Library /
Press, 1972-1973). One hundred and fifty copies
[numbered at the press].)

F. The Poetry of Thomas Merton in Periodicals, Newspapers and Books

Arranged chronologically

The following abbreviations are used: TP (Thirty Poems); AMITDS (A Man in the Divided Sea); FFAA (Figures for an Apocalypse); TTOTBL (The Tears of the Blind Lions); TSI (The Strange Islands); EOASOF (Emblems of a Season of Fury); CTTA (Cables to the Ace), and TGOL (The Geography of Lograire).

(In the main body of the bibliography the only allusion to Merton's poetry was in listing and describing his eight books of verse: A1: *Thirty Poems*; A2: *A Man in the Divided Sea*; A5: *Figures for an Apocalypse*; A12: *The Tears of the Blind Lions*; A25: *The Strange Islands*; A41: *Emblems of a Season of Fury*; A51: *Cables to the Ace*; A57: *The Geography of Lograire*; E2: *Selected Poems of Thomas Merton*. On advisement I did not list the individual appearance of his poems which, began appearing in anthologies, newspapers and magazines from 1939 to 1955, but immediately after publication of the bibliography in *Thought* (*Fordham University Quarterly*, XXIX. 115 (Winter, 1954-1955) [574]-596) a separate listing of Merton's verse was deemed essential to the bibliographical researcher and thesis writer.)

F1 "Fable for a War"; "Aubade: Bermuda"; "Litany";
"Bureaucrats: Diggers"; "These Years a Winter";
"Christmas as to People." In *Columbia Poetry* [an anthology
of Columbia students' verse], with an Introduction by
Charles Hanson Towne. New York: Columbia University
Press (June 1939); pp. 60-61, 62, 63, 64, 65, 66-67.
(None of these poems appear in his books of poetry.)
    "Fable for a War" won for the author (June 1939), a
graduate student of the Faculty of Philosophy, the annual Mariana
Griswold van Rensselaer prize for the best example of English
lyric verse.

F2 [Second appearance of] "Fable for a War" (excerpt:
Columbia Poetry; see F1). *The New York Times*
(June 18, 1939) 36:6.

F3 [First appearance of] "Song" (in AMITDS).
Experimental Review, 2 (November 1940), 38.
(Defunct.)

F4 [First appearance of]" A Meditation on Christ's Passion"
(in TP; all poems in TP were later (August 25, 1946)
published in AMITDS; pp. 113-155; see A2; in both
volumes poem reads: "An Argument: Of the Passion of
Christ"). *Spirit*, VIII. 2 (May 1941) 44-45.

F5 [First appearance of] "Lent in a Year of War" (in TP &
AMITDS). *View*, 1. 6 (June 1941) [a leaf insert between
pp. 2 & 3]. (Defunct.)

F6 [First appearance of] "The Sponge Full of Vinegar"
(in TP & AMITDS). *Spirit*, VIII. 3 (July 1941) 80.

F7 [First appearance of] "The Trappist Abbey: Matins"
(in TP & AMITDS). *Spirit*, VIII. 4 (September 1941) 111.

F8 [First appearance of] "The Flight into Egypt" (in TP & AMITDS). *Spirit*, VIII. 5 (November 1941) 148.

F9 [First appearance of] "The Night Train," "The Dark Morning" (in TP & AMITDS); "Poem: 1941" (in AMITDS; verse here reads: "Poem: 1939"), "Dirge" (in AMITDS). *Poetry*, LX. 1 (April 1942) 20-23.

F10 [First appearance of] "Aubade: Lake Erie" (in TP & AMITDS). *The New Yorker*, XVIII. 24 (August 1, 1942) 27.

F11 [Second appearance of] "The Winter's Night," "The Regret" (first appearance in TP); [First appearance of] "Ash Wednesday," "Ariadne," "Some Bloody Mutiny," "The Greek Women" (in AMITDS). *The Quarterly Review of Literature*, 1. 2 (Winter 1944) 76-80.

F12 [Second appearance of] "The Sponge Full of Vinegar" (see F6), "The Trappist Abbey: Matins" (see F7) (in TP & AMITDS). In *Drink From the Rock, Selected Poems from* Spirit, *a Magazine of Poetry*, with an Introduction by Helen C. White, PhD. New York: The Catholic Poetry Society of America, Incorporated (April 1944); pp. 66, 71.

F13 [First appearance of] "Carol" (in AMITDS). *The New Yorker*, XX. 45 (December 23, 1944) 36.

F14 [Second appearance of] "The Vine" (in TP & AMITDS). *The Catholic Art Quarterly*, VIII. 2 (Easter 1945) 28.

F15 [Second appearance of] "For My Brother: Reported Missing in Action, 1943" (in TP & AMITDS). *The Catholic Art Quarterly*, VIII. 2 (Easter 1945) 29.

F16 [Second appearance of] "Death" (in TP & AMITDS).
The Catholic Art Quarterly, VIII. 3 (Pentecost 1945) 15.

F17 [First appearance of] "Two States of Prayer" (in FFAA).
Voices, 124 (Winter 1946), 23-24.

F18 [First appearance of] "Fugitive," "The Ohio River:
Louisville," "After the Night Office: Gethsemani Abbey"
(in AMITDS). *Chimera*, IV. 2 (Winter 1946) 2-4.
(Defunct.)

F19 [Fifth appearance of] "The Trappist Abbey: Matins"
(see F7, F12) (in TP & AMITDS); [Fourth appearance
of] "For My Brother" (see F15) (in TP & AMITDS).
In *A New Anthology of Modern Poetry* (Revised
Edition), edited, and with an Introduction, by Selden
Rodman. New York, The Modern Library (December
1946); pp. 420-421, 422-423. (A Modern Library
Giant, ♯G46.)

F20 [Second appearance of] "Two States of Prayer" (see F17)
(in FFAA); [First appearance of] "On the Anniversary
of my Baptism" (in FFAA). *The Commonweal*, XLIII.
26 (April 12, 1946) 640.

F21 [First appearance of] "Duns Scotus" (in FFAA). *The
Commonweal*, XLV. 16 (January 31, 1947) 397.

F21a [Third appearance of] "The Blessed Virgin Compared
to a Window," "The Evening of the Visitation" (in TP
& AMITDS). In *I Sing of a Maiden (The Mary Book of
Verse)*, ed. Sister M. Therese. New York: The Macmillan
Company (no month; 1947); pp. 354-355, 356.

F22 [First appearance of] "A Letter to America" (in FFAA).
The Commonweal, XLV. 17 (February 7, 1947) 419.

F23 [First appearance of] "Landscape: Wheatfields" (in
FFAA). *The Commonweal*, XLV. 19 (February 21,
1947) 463.

F24 [First appearance of] "In the Ruins of New York"
(in FFAA). *The Commonweal*, XLVI. 8 (June 6,
1947) 182.

F25 [First appearance of] "Canticle for the Blessed Virgin"
(in FFAA). *The Commonweal*, XLVI. 16
(August 1, 1947) 375.

F26 [First appearance of] "Landscape," "Prophet and
Wild-Dog" (in FFAA). *The Western Review*, 12. 1
(Autumn 1947) [30]-31.

F27 [First appearance of] "The Landfall" (in FFAA).
The Tiger's Eye, 1. 1 (October 1947) 1-2. (Defunct).

F28 [Second appearance of] "On the Anniversary of my
Baptism" (see F20) (in FFAA). *The Sewanee Review*,
LV. 4 (October 1947; Autumn) [648]-649.

F29 [First appearance of] "Natural History" (in FFAA).
The Commonweal, XLVI. 26 (October 10, 1947) 614.

F30 [First appearance of] "Theory of Prayer" (in FFAA).
The Commonweal, XLVII. 2 (October 24, 1947) 40.

F31 [First appearance of] "Evening: Zero Weather" (in
FFAA). *Spirit*, XIV. 5 (November 1947) 126-127.

F32 [First appearance of] "Clairvaux Prison" (in FFAA).
The Catholic Worker, XIV. 10 (January 1948) 5:1.

F33 [First appearance of] "On a Day in August" (in
TTOTBL). *Epoch*, 1. 2 (Winter 1948) 58-59.

F34 [First appearance of] "St. Jerome" (in FFAA). *Spirit*, XIV. 6 (January 1948) 159.

F35 [Third appearance of] "Poem: 1939" (see A2, F9); [Second appearance of] "The Oracle," "The Betrayal" (see A2); [Fifth appearance of] "The Sponge Full of Vinegar" (see A2, F6, F12); [Fourth appearance of] "The Evening of the Visitation" (see A2, F21a) (excerpt: *A Man in the Divided Sea*). In *Return to Tradition (A Directive Anthology)*, ed. Francis B. Thornton, [S.J.]. Milwaukee, The Bruce Publishing Company (April 1948); pp. 851-852.

F36 [First appearance of] "The Quickening of St. John the Baptist" (in TTOTBL). *Spirit*, XV. 2 (May 1948) 48-50.

F37 [First appearance of] "A Psalm" (in TTOTBL). *The Commonweal*, XLVIII. 5 (May 14, 1948) 95.

F38 [First appearance of] "Messias" (not included in his volumes of verse). *Spirit*, XV. 3 (July 1948) 70-71.

F39 [First appearance of] "To the Immaculate Virgin, on a Winter Night" (in TTOTBL). *The Commonweal*, XLVIII. 17 (August 6, 1948) 399.

F40 [First appearance of] "Song" (in TTOTBL). *Horizon*, XVIII. 105 (September 1948) [153]. (Defunct.)

F41 [First appearance of] "Dry Places" (in TTOTBL). *The Hudson Review*, 1. 3 (Autumn 1948) [340-341].

F42 [Fifth appearance of] ["For My Brother: Reported Missing in Action, 1943"] (see F15, F19) (in TP & AMITDS). In *The Seven Storey Mountain*, by Thomas Merton. New York: Harcourt, Brace and Company (October 1948), p. 404.

F42a [Third appearance of] ["Song for Our Lady of Cobre"] (in TP & AMITDS). In *The Seven Storey Mountain*, by Thomas Merton. New York: Harcourt, Brace and Company (October 1948), p. 283.

F43 [First appearance of] "From the Legend of St. Clement" (in TTOTBL). *The Month*, 1. 1 (January 1949) [5]-6.

F44 [First appearance of] "St. Malachy" (in TTOTBL); [Second appearance of] "From the Legend of St. Clement" (see F43) (in TTOTBL). *Poetry*, 73. 5 (February 1949) 255-258.

F45 [First appearance of] "A Responsory, 1948" (in TTOTBL). *The Partisan Review*, XVI. 3 (March 1949) 269-270.

F46 [Third appearance of] "A Letter to America"; "Landscape: Wheatfields" (see A5, F22, F23) (excerpt: *Figures for an Apocalypse*). In the *Commonweal Reader*, ed. Edward S. Skillin. New York: Harper & Brothers (September 1949), pp. 288-289, 297-298.

F47 [First appearance of] "Like Ilium" (not included in his volumes of verse). *Spirit*, XVI. 5 (November 1949) 135.

F48 [First appearance of] "Hymn for the Feast of Duns Scotus;" "Reader" (in TTOTBL). *The Atlantic Monthly*, 184. 6 (December 1949) [54-55].

F49 [Sixth appearance of] "For My Brother/Sgt. John Paul Merton, R.C.A.F./Reported Misssing in Action, 1943" (see F15, F19, F42) (in TP & AMITDS). In *A Second Treasury of the Familiar*, ed. Ralph L. Woods. New York: The Macmillan Company (April 1950), pp. 519-520.

F50 [Third appearance of] "Evening: Zero Weather" (see A5,
F31); "The Quickening of St. John the Baptist" (see A12,
F36); [Second appearance of] "Messias" (see F38).
In *From One Word, Selected Poems from "Spirit"*
1944-1949, ed. John Gilland Brunini. New York: The
Devin-Adair Company (December 1950), pp. 80-81,
96-98, 112-114.

F51 [Seventh appearance of] "For My Brother:/Reported
Missing in Action, 1943" (see F15, F19, F42, F49)
in TP & AMITDS). In *Introduction to Poetry*, ed.
Mark Van Doren. New York: William Sloane Associates,
Incorporated (February 1951), pp. 530-531.

F52 [Eighth appearance of] ["For My Brother: Reported
Missing in Action, 1943"] (see F15, F19, F42, F49, F51)
in TP & AMITDS). In *The Seven Storey Mountain*
(Reprint edition; see A7, b), by Thomas Merton. New
York: Garden City Books (February 1951), p. 404.

F52a [Fourth appearance of] ["Song for Our Lady of Cobre"]
(see F42a) (in TP & AMITDS). In *The Seven Storey
Mountain* (Reprint edition; see A7, b), by Thomas Merton.
New York: Garden City Books (February 1951), p. 283.

F53 [Ninth appearance of] "For My Brother:/Reported
Missing in Action, 1943" (see F15, F19, F42, F49, F51,
F52) (in TP & AMITDS). In *Enjoying Poetry*, ed.
Mark Van Doren. New York: William Sloane Associates,
Incorporated (July 1951), pp. 530-531.

F54 [Second appearance of] "A Christmas Card" (in FFAA).
Perspectives USA/Pilot Issue (January 1952) [192].

F55 [Second appearance of] "Sports Without Blood/A Letter to [the late] Dylan Thomas." *In New World Writing/ First Mentor Selection* (♯Ms 73). New York: The New American Library of World Literature, Incorporated (April 1952), pp. 74-77.

This poem first appeared in England in 1950 in a volume entitled: Selected Poems of Thomas Merton; see E2. It appears here in an abridged and edited form.

F56 [First appearance of] "Early Mass" (St. Joseph Infirmary-Louisville) (in TSI). *The Commonweal*, LVI. 2 (April 18, 1952) 48.

F57 [Scattered quotes from the essay:] "Poetry and the Contemplative Life" [which is included as a supplement to] *Figures for an Apocalypse* (see A5, B3, C14); [a brief critical piece relative to Merton's poetry;] [an analytical summary of] "The Communion" (in TP & AMITDS) [third appearance of this poem which contains four stanzas but here the third stanza is omitted; also mentioned in the discussion but not quoted are the following poems:] "To My Brother Reported Missing in Action," and "In Memory of the Spanish Poet, Lorca" (in TP & AMITDS); [also quoted (third appearance) is the epitaph stanza of] "In The Ruins of New York" (see F24) (in FFAA); "The Captives: A Psalm" (in TTOTBL) [second appearance of this poem which contains seven stanzas but here only stanza four, five and seven are quoted;] [a brief analysis of Merton's verse, plus a single line quotation from] "Death" (in TP & AMITDS), [stanza five, line two]. In *Modern Poetry and the Christian Tradition* (A study in the relation of Christianity to culture), by Amos N. Wilder. New York: Charles Scribner's Sons (April 1952), pp. 13, 114, 115, 141-143, 208, 209.

150

F58 [Tenth appearance of] ["For My Brother: Reported Missing in Action, 1943"] (see F15, F19, F42, F49, F51, F52, F53) (in TP & AMITDS). In *The Seven Storey Mountain* (Paper-back edition; see A7, c), by Thomas Merton. [New York:] The New American Library (April 1952), p. 484.

F58a [Fifth appearance of] ["Song for Our Lady of Cobre"] (see F42a, F52a) (in TP & AMITDS). In *The Seven Storey Mountain* (Paper-back edition; see A7, c), by Thomas Merton. [New York:] The New American Library (April 1952), p. 277 (pagination refers to Sixteenth Printing).

F59 [First appearance of] "Christmas, 1951" (For the Carmelites) (not included in his volumes of verse). *The Commonweal*, LVII. 12 (December 26, 1952) 307.

F60 [First appearance of] ["A Prelude: For the Feast of St. Agnes."] In *The Sign of Jonas*, by Thomas Merton. New York: Harcourt, Brace and Company (February 1953); p. 270.

F61 [Fourth appearance of] "Poeme: 1939" (see F9, F35) (in AMITDS). *Profils*, 4 (Juillet 1953) 33.

F62 [Second appearance of] "Like Ilium" (see F47); [Fourth appearance of] "Two States of Prayer" (see F17, F20) (in FFAA); [Second appearance of] "Ode to the Present Century" (in AMITDS); [Third appearance of] "Messias" (see F38, F50). In *Joyce Kilmer's Anthology of Catholic Poets*, with a new supplement by James Edward Tobin. New York: Image Books (♯ D15)-A division of Doubleday & Company, Incorporated (February 1955), pp. 321-325.

F63 [Eleventh appearance of] "For My Brother: Reported Missing in Action, 1943" (see F15, F19, F42, F49, F51, F52, F53, F58) (in TP & AMITDS). In *The American Treasury* (1455-1955), selected, arranged, and edited by Clifton Fadiman, assisted by Charles Van Doren. New York: Harper & Brothers (November 1955), pp. 616-617. (This poem has five stanzas but here only stanza four and five are quoted.)

F64 [Second appearance of] "A Prelude: For the Feast of St. Agnes" (see F60). *The Commonweal*, LXIII. 12 (December 23, 1955) 304.

F65 [Third appearance of] "A Prelude: For the Feast of St. Agnes" (see F60, F64). *Pax*, 1 (1956) unpaged.

F66 [Fourth appearance of] ["A Prelude: For the Feast of St. Agnes"] (see F60, F64, F65). In *The Sign of Jonas* (Paper-back edition; see A17, b), by Thomas Merton. New York: Image Books (♯D31)-A division of Doubleday & Company, Incorporated (February 1956), pp. 263-264.

F67 [Second appearance of] "Annunciation" (original title: Christmas, 1951—For the Carmelites) (see F59); [First appearance of] "Stranger" (both poems in TSI). *The Sign*, 35. 8 (March 1956) 31.

F68 [First appearance of] "Elias: Variations on a Theme" (in TSI). *Thought*, XXXI. 121 (Summer 1956) [245]-250.

F69 [Fourth appearance of] "An Argument: On the Passion of Christ" (see F4) (in TP & AMITDS); [Second appearance of] "Landscape: Beast" (in FFAA). In *The Criterion Book of Modern American Verse*, edited with an introduction by W. H. Auden. New York: Criterion Books (November 1956), pp. 284-286, 286-287.

F70 [First appearance of] "Sincerity" (in TSI). *Poetry*, LXXXIX. 3 (December 1956) 140-141.

F71 [Third appearance of] "St. Agnes: A Responsory" (in TP & AMITDS). In *The Mentor Book of Religious Verse*, ed. Horace Gregory and Maya Zaturenska. New York: A Mentor Book (Published by The New American Library) (January 1957), p. 169.

F72 [First appearance of] "Wisdom," "Birdcage Walk," "Landscape," "Nocturne" (in TSI), "Song: In the Shows of the Round Ox" (in SPOTM). *Pax*, 4 (1957) unpaged.

F73 [Second appearance of] "The Guns of Fort Knox" (in TSI). *The Sign*, 37. 1 (August 1957) 39.

F74 [Second appearance of] "To the Immaculate Virgin, on a Winter Night" (in TTOTBL). *Book News* (Stechert-Hafner), XII. 4 (December 1957) 42.

F75 [First appearance of] "A Practical Program for Monks," "An Elegy for Five Old Ladies" (in SPOTM). *Pax*, 7 (1958) unpaged.

F76 [Second appearance of] "Programa practico para monjes" (see F75) (in SPOTM). *El Colombiand* (Agosto 10, 1958) unpaged.

F77 [Third appearance of] "A Psalm" (see F37) (in TTOTBL). *The Commonweal*, LXIX. 4 (October 24, 1958) 89.

F78 [Sixth appearance of] "The Trappist Abbey: Matins" (see F7, F12, F19) (in TP & AMITDS). In *Poetry for Pleasure (The Hallmark Book of Poetry)*, selected and arranged by the editors of Hallmark Cards. New York: Doubleday & Company (no month; 1959), p. 360.

F79 [Sixth appearance of] "Preludium: Na uroczystosc swietej Agnieszki" (see F60, F64, F65, F66) (in TSI). *Slowo Powszechne*, 45 (October 24-25, 1959) 2.

F80 [First appearance of] "Love Winter When the Plant Says Nothing" (in EOASOF). *The Catholic Worker*, XXVI. 11 (June 1960) 4:4.

F81 [First appearance of] "Chant to be Used in Processions Around a Site with Furnaces" (in EOASOF). *Journal for the Protection of all Beings*, 1 (Love-Shot Issue) (1961) 5-7.

F82 [First appearance of] "A Messenger from the Horizon" (in EOASOF). *The Saturday Review*, XLIV. 6 (February 11, 1961) 40.

F83 [First appearance of] "Song for Nobody" (in EOASOF). *The Saturday Review*, XLIV. 29 (July 22, 1961) 21.

F84 [Second appearance of] "Chant to be Used in Processions Around a Site with Furnaces" (see F81) (in EOASOF). *The Catholic Worker*, XXVIII. 1 (July-August 1961) 4:3.

F85 [First appearance of] "An Elegy for Ernest Hemingway" (in EOASOF). *The Commonweal*, LXXIV. 21 (September 22, 1961) 513.

F86 [Second appearance of] "Elegia a la Muerte de Hemingway" (see F85) (in EOASOF). *El Universal* (Caracas). (January 23, 1962) unpaged.

F86a [First appearance of] "Advice to a Young Prophet." *The Catholic Worker*, XXVIII. 6 (January 1962) 4:2.

F87 [First appearance of] "The Moment of Truth" (not included in his volumes of verse). *The Critic*, XX. 4 (March 1962) 21.

F88 [Third appearance of] "Chant to be Used in Processions Around a Site with Furnaces" (see F81, F84) (in EOASOF). *Blackfriars*, XLIII. 502 (April 1962) 180-182.

F89 [First appearance of] "The Moslems' Angel of Death" (in EOASOF). *The Commonweal*, LXXVI. 10 (June 1, 1962) 255.

F90 [First appearance of] "Elegy for James Thurber" (in EOASOF). *The Commonweal*, LXXVI. 16 (July 13, 1962) 396.

F91 [First appearance of] "Seven Archaic Images" (in EOASOF). *The Saturday Review*, XLV. 31 (August 4, 1962) 24.

F92 [Sixth appearance of] ["Song for Our Lady of Cobre"] (see F42a, F52a, F58a) (in TP & AMITDS). In *A Thomas Merton Reader*, ed. Thomas P. McDonnell. New York: Harcourt, Brace & World (October 24, 1962), pp. 74-75.

F93 [First appearance of] "Song for the Death of Averroes" (in EOASOF). *The Texas Quarterly*, V. 4 (Winter 1962) 61-63.

F94 [Third appearance of] "Landscape: Beast" (see F69) (in FFAA); [Second appearance of] "Song" (in AMITDS); [Fourth appearance of] "Lent in a Year of War" (see F5) (in TP & AMITDS); [Fourth appearance of] "The Flight Into Egypt" (see F8) (in TP & AMITDS); [Fourth appearance of] "The Night Train" (see F9) (in TP & AMITDS); [Fourth appearance of] "Aubade: Lake Erie" (see F10) (in TP & AMITDS); [Third appearance of] "Ash Wednesday" (see F11) (in AMITDS); [Third appearance of] "An Elegy for Ernest Hemingway" (see F85, F86) (in EOASOF); [Third appearance of] "Landscape" (see F72) (in TSI); [Second appearance of] "Aubade: Harlem" (in AMITDS); [Third appearance of] "Dirge for the Proud World" (in TP & AMITDS); [Fifth appearance of] "An Argument: Of the Passion of Christ" (see F4, F69) (in TP & AMITDS); [Second appearance of] "Crusoe" (in AMITDS); [Second appearance of] "The Bombarded City" (in AMITDS); [Second appearance of] "Song" (in AMITDS); [Twelfth appearance of] "For My Brother: Reported Missing in Action, 1943" (see F15, F19, F42, F49, F51, F52, F53, F58, F63) (in TP & AMITDS); [Second appearance of] "The Trappist Cemetery: Gethsemani" (in AMITDS); [Seventh appearance of] "The Trappist Abbey: Matins" (see F7, F12, F19, F78) (in TP & AMITDS); [Fourth appearance of] "Evening: Zero Weather" (see F36, F50) (in FFAA); [Third appearance of] "After the Night Office: Gethsemani Abbey" (see F18) (in AMITDS); [Third appearance of] "The Reader" (see F48) (in TTOTBL); [Third appearance of] "St. Malachy" (see F44) (in TTOTBL); [Second appearance of] "Elegy for the Monastery Barn" (in TSI); [Fourth appearance of] "A Practical Program for Monks" (see F75, F76) (in SPOTM); [Second appearance of] "Freedom as Experience" (in FFAA); [Second appearance of] "Cana" (in AMITDS); [Third appearance of] "Evening" (in TP & AMITDS); [Fourth appearance of] "The Annunciation" (see F59, F67) (in TSI); [Second appearance of] "A Psalm" (in TTOTBL); [Fourth appearance of] "The Quickening of St. John the Baptist" (see F36, F50) (in TTOTBL); [Fifth appearance of] "Chant to be Used in Processions Around a Site with Furnaces" (see F81, F84, F88) (in

156

EOASOF); [Third appearance of] "The Landfall"
(see F27) (in FFAA); [Second appearance of] "The
Sowing of Meanings" (in FFAA); [Third appearance of]
"Stranger" (see F67) (in TSI); [Seventh appearance of]
"A Prelude: for the Feast of St. Agnes" (see F60, F64,
F65, F66, F79) (in TSI); [Third appearance of] "A
Responsory, 1948" (see F45) (in TTOTBL); [Third
appearance of] "The Captives: A Psalm" (see F57)
(in TTOTBL); [Second appearance of] "Senescente
Mundo" (in TTOTBL); [Second appearance of] "In the
Rain and the Sun" (in TTOTBL); [Third appearance
of] "Wisdom" (see F72) (in TSI); [Third appearance
of] "Elias: Variations on a Theme" (see F68) (in TSI);
[Second appearance of] " 'When in the Soul of the Serene
Disciple . . .' " (in TSI); [Second appearance of] "Spring
Storm" (in TSI); [Second appearance of] "Dry Places"
(in TTOTBL); [Second appearance of] "The Heavenly
City" (in FFAA). In *A Thomas Merton Reader*, ed.
Thomas P. McDonnell. New York: Harcourt, Brace &
World (October 24, 1962), pp. 32-39, 107-114, 171-181,
366-372, 404-406, 451-458, 516-526.

F95 [First appearance of] "Why Some Look up to Planets
and Heroes" (in EOASOF). *America*, CVIII. 13 (March
30, 1963) 433. (Alongside poem a comment by
Thomas Merton.)

F96 [First appearance of] "A Picture of Lee Ying," "Gloss
on the Sin of Ixion" (in EOASOF). *El Corno Emplumado*,
6 (April 1963) 8-14.

F97 [First appearance of] "After Chuang Tzu." *El Corno
Emplumado*, 6 (April 1963) 14-16. (This poem later
appeared in *The Way of Chuang Tzu* (see A43)
entitled: "The Useless Tree" (35-36).)

F97a [First appearance of] "To Alfonso Cortes."
Continuum, I. 2 (Spring 1963) 76.

F98 [Sixth appearance of] "Chant to be Used in Processions
Around a Site with Furnaces" (see F81, F84, F88, F94)
(in EOASOF). *Fellowship*, 29. 5 (July 1963) 26-27.

F99 [First appearance of] "And the Children of Birmingham"
(in EOASOF). *The Saturday Review*, XLVI. 32
(August 10, 1963) 32.

F100 [Second appearance of] "Cancion para ninguno"
(see F83); [First appearance of] "Y asi adios a las
ciudades" ("And So Goodbye to Cities") (in EOASOF).
Eco Contemporaneo, 6/7 (1963) 92, 92-93.

F101 [Second appearance of] "Gloss on the Sin of Ixion"
(see F96) (in EOASOF). *The Saturday Review*,
46. 38 (September 21, 1963) 29.

F101a [First appearance of] "The Fall." *Continuum*, I. 3
(Autumn 1963) 386.

F102 [First appearance of] "A Baroque Gravure" (not
included in his volumes of verse). *The Commonweal*,
LXXIX. 6 (November 1, 1963) 167.

F103 [First appearance of] "Seneca" (not included in his
volumes of verse). *Poetry*, 103. 6 (March 1964) 381.

F104 [First appearance of] "Picture of a Negro Child
with a White Doll" (not included in his volumes of verse).
New Blackfriars, 46. 532 (October 1964) [32].

F105 [Third appearance of] "Elegy for the Monastery Barn"
(see F94) (in TSI). *The Sign*, 44. 3 (October 1964) [49].

F106 [Fourth appearance of] "Stranger" (see F67, F94) (in TSI). In *The Earth is the Lord's (Poems of the Spirit)*, comp. Helen Plotz. New York: Thomas Y. Crowell Company (no month; 1965), pp. 14-15.

F107 [Third appearance of] "Duns Scotus" (see F21) (in FFAA); [Fourth appearance of] "St. Malachy" (see F44, F94) (in TTOTBL); [Fourth appearance of] "Elegy for the Monastery Barn" (see F94, F105) (in TSI); [Second appearance of] "To a Severe Nun" (in TSI); [Fifth appearance of] "A Practical Program for Monks" (see F75, F76, F94) (in SPOTM); [Second appearance of] "A Baroque Gravure" (see F102) (not included in his volumes of verse); [Second appearance of] "Seneca" (see F103) (not included in his volumes of verse). In *A Controversy of Poets (An Anthology of Contemporary American Poetry)*, ed. Paris Leary and Robert Kelly. New York: Doubleday & Company (Anchor Books, ♯A439) (no month; 1965), pp. [273]-281.

F108 [First appearance of] "For the Spanish Poet: Miguel Hernandez" (not included in his volumes of verse). *The Sewanee Review*, LXXIV. 4 (October-December 1966) 897-898.

F109 [First appearance of] "Elegy for a Trappist" (not included in his volumes of verse). *The Commonweal*, LXXXV. 10 (December 9, 1966) 294.

F110 [First appearance of] "Epitaph for a Public Servant" (not included in his volumes of verse). *Motive*, XXVII. 8 (May 1967) 16-17.

F111 [First appearance of] "Early Blizzard" (not included in his volumes of verse), [First appearance of] "Sweetgum

Avenue Leads to a College of Charm" (in CTTA),
[First appearance of] "Lion" (not included in his volumes
of verse), [First appearance of] "Rain and Vision,"
"The Harmonies of Excess," "The Planet Over Eastern
Parkway" (in CTTA). *The Sewanee Review*, LXXV. 3
(July-September 1967) [385]-392.

F112 [First appearance of] "North" (in TGOL). *Monks
Pond*, 1 (Spring 1968) 26-31.

F113 [First appearance of] "Found Macaronic Antipoem"
(from an Elementary Reader, Augsburg, 1514) (not
included in his volumes of verse). *Monks Pond*, 2
(Summer 1968) unpaged.

F114 [First appearance of] "Why I Have a Wet Footprint
on Top of My Mind" (in TGOL). *Cimarron Review*,
4 (June 1968) 31.

F115 [First appearance of] "Notes for a New Liturgy"
(in TGOL). *Poetry*, 112. 4 (July 1968) 254-255.

F116 [First appearance of] "Hopeless and Felons" (not
included in his volumes of verse). *Cimarron Review*, 5
(September 1968) 68.

F117 [Untitled poem.] *Monks Pond*, 3 (Fall 1968) unpaged.

F118 [First appearance of] "The Geography of Lograire/
Prologue: The Endless Inscription" (in TGOL).
Monks Pond, 3 (Fall 1968) 42-44.

F118a [First appearance of] "The Ladies of Tlatilco"
(in TGOL). *Green River Review*, I. 1
(November 1968) 23-25.

F119 [Untitled poem.] *Monks Pond*, 4 (Winter 1968)
unpaged.

160

F120 [First appearance of] "Semiotic Poem from Racine's Iphigenia" (not included in his volumes of verse). *Monks Pond*, 4 (Winter 1968) unpaged.

F121 [First appearance of] "African Religious Myths" (in TGOL). *Monks Pond*, 4 (Winter 1968) 73.

F122 [First appearance of] "Proverbs" (for Robert Lax) (not included in his volumes of verse). *Monks Pond*, 4 (Winter 1968) 85-86.

F123 [First appearance of] Scattered, untitled excerpts from TGOL. *Monks Pond*, 5 (Winter 1968) 87-89.

F124 [Fifth appearance of] "[Two States of] Prayer" (see F17, F20, F62) (in FFAA); [Fourth appearance of] "[On the Anniversary of my] Baptism" (see F20, F28) (in FFAA); [Fourth appearance of] "[An Elegy for] Ernest Hemingway" (see F85, F86, F94) (in EOASOF). *The Commonweal*, LXXXIX. 13 (December 27, 1968) 435, 435, 436.

F125 [First appearance of] "Tibud Maclay" (in TGOL). *The Outsider*, 2. 4/5 (Winter 1968-1969) 158-159.

F126 [First appearance of] "First Lesson About Man" (not included in his volumes of verse). *The Saturday Review*, LII. 2 (January 11, 1969) 21.

F127 [Fifth appearance of] "Aubade: Lake Erie" (see F10, F94) (in TP & AMITDS). In *The New Yorker Book of Poems*, selected by the editors of *The New Yorker*. New York: The Viking Press (no month; 1969), p. 39.

F128 [Seventh appearance of] ["Song for Our Lady of Cobre"] (see F42a, F52a, F58a, F92) (in TP &

AMITDS); [Thirteenth appearance of] ["For My
Brother: Reported Missing in Action, 1943"] (see F15,
F19, F42, F49, F51, F52, F53, F58, F63, F94) (in TP &
AMITDS). In *The Seven Storey Mountain* (Paper-back
edition; see A7, d), by Thomas Merton. New York:
Image Books (♯ D281)-A division of Doubleday &
Company, Incorporated (September 1970),
pp. 342-343, 489.

F129 [Second appearance of] "Elegy for Father Stephen"
(original title: "Elegy for a Trappist"; see F109)
(not included in his volumes of verse). *Sisters Today*, 42.
2 (October 1970) 74.

F129a [Fourteenth appearance of] "For My Brother:
Reported Missing in Action 1943" (see F15, F19, F42,
F49, F51, F52, F53, F58, F63, F94, F128) (in TP &
AMITDS). In *Who Am I?: Second Thoughts on Man,
His Loves and His Gods*, ed. Lowell D. Streiker.
New York: Sheed and Ward (no month; 1970),
pp. 80-81.

F130 [Third appearance of] "The Holy Child's Song" (in
TP & AMITDS). *Vogue*, 156. 10 (December 1970) 112.

F131 [First appearance of] "Origen" (not included in
his volumes of verse). *Monastic Studies*, 8
(Spring 1972) 117-118.

F132 [Second appearance of] "Prayer to Saint Anatole,"
"I am About to Make My Home" (in CTTA). In *Toward
Winter (Poems For The Last Decade)*, ed. Robert
Bonazzi. New York: A New Rivers/Latitudes Press Book
(no month; 1972), pp. 66, 67.

G. Translations into Foreign Languages of Books, Poems and Essays by Thomas Merton

Arranged alphabetically by language and chronologically by title

CHINESE

G1 *Me Kuan Sheng Huo T'an Pi.* Taichung: Kuang Chi Press, 1959. A translation, by Chiang Ping-lun, of *Seeds of Contemplation.*

DANISH

G2 *Den Store Stilhed.* København: Arne Frost—Hansens Forlag, 1950. A translation, by Kay Nielsen, of *The Seven Storey Mountain.*

G3 *Stilhedens Forjaettelse.* København: Arne Frost—Hansens Forlag, 1952. A translation, by Ebba Friis Hansen, of *Seeds of Contemplation.*

G4 *Jonastegnet.* København: Arne Frost—Hansens Forlag, 1955. A translation, by Anna Sofie Scavenius, of *The Sign of Jonas.*

164

DUTCH

G5 *Van Ballingschap en Overwinning.* Antwerpen: Sheed & Ward, 1949. A translation, by Jook Steenhoff, of *Exile Ends in Glory* [contains a new Introduction by Thomas Merton].

G6 *De Roep Der Wonden.* Antwerpen: Sheed & Ward, 1950. A translation, by Maria Theunen, of *What Are These Wounds?* [Contains an Introduction by the translator.]

G7 *Louteringsberg.* Holland: Het Spectrum, 1950. A translation, by Andre Noorbeek, of *The Seven Storey Mountain.*

G8 *De Wateren Van Siloe.* Holland: Het Spectrum, 1950. A translation, by Andre Noorbeek, of *The Waters of Siloe.*

G9 *Ter Overweging.* Holland: Het Spectrum, 1952. A translation, by Andre Noorbeek, of *Seeds of Contemplation.*

G10 *De Berg Der Waarheid.* Antwerpen: Sheed & Ward, 1953. A translation, by J. Depres, of *The Ascent to Truth.*

G11 *Overpeinzingen Van Een Christen.* Utrecht: Spectrum, 1966. A translation, by Cyprianus van den Bogaard, of *Life and Holiness.*

FLEMISH

G12 *Louteringsberg.* Brussels: Uitgeverij Het Spectrum, 1951. A translation, by Andre Noorbeek, of *The Seven Storey Mountain.*

G13 *De Wateren Van Siloe.* Brussels: Uitgeverij Het Spectrum, 1951. A translation, by Andre Noorbeek, of *The Waters of Siloe.*

G14 *Aux Sources Du Silence.* Brugge: Desclee de Brouwer, 1954. A translation, by Jean Stienon du Pre, of *The Waters of Siloe.*

G15 *Quelles Sont Ces Plaies?* Brugge: Desclee de Brouwer, 1954. A translation, by a Dominican Nun, of *What Are These Wounds?*

G15a *Ter Overweging.* Antwerpen: Uitgeverij Het Spectrum, 1954. A translation, by Andre Noorbeek, of *Seeds of Contemplation.*

G16 *Uw Naaste Als Uzelf.* Antwerpen: Het Spectrum, 1957. A translation, by J. K. van den Brink, of *No Man Is An Island.*

G17 *L'Exil S'Acheve dans la Gloire.* Brugge: Desclee de Brouwer, 1958. A translation of *Exile Ends in Glory.*

G18 *Brood in de Woestjin.* Tongerlo-Antwerpen: Sint-Norbertus-Boekhandel, 1958. A translation of *Bread in the Wilderness.*

G19 *Levend Brood.* Brugge: Desclee de Brouwer, 1958. A translation, by J. Boosman, of *The Living Bread.*

G20 *Louteringsberg.* Merksem, Westland, 1959. A translation, by Andre Noorbeek, of *The Seven Storey Mountain.*

G21 *Het Stille Leven.* Brugge: Desclee de Brouwer, 1961. A translation of *The Silent Life.*

G22 *Le Temps des Fetes.* Tournai: Castermann, 1968. A translation, by Marie Tadie, of *Seasons of Celebration.*

G23 *Oplettende Toeschouwer.* Brugge: Desclee de Brouwer, 1969. A translation, by Martha van de Walle, of *Conjectures of a Guilty Bystander.*

FRENCH

G24 *La Nuit Privee D'etoiles.* Paris: Editions Albin Michel, 1951. A translation, by Marie Tadie, of *The Seven Storey Mountain.*

G25 *Semences de Contemplation.* Paris: Aux Editions du Seuil, 1952. A translation, by R. N. Raimbault, of *Seeds of Contemplation.*

G26 *Aux Sources du Silence.* Paris: Desclee de Brouwer, 1952. A translation, by Jean Stienon du Pre, of *The Waters of Siloe.*

G27 *Quelles Sont Ces Plaies?* Paris: Desclee de Brouwer, 1953. A translation, by a Dominican Nun, of *What Are These Wounds?* [Contains a Preface by P. Benoit Lavaud, O.P.]

G28 *La Manne du Desert ou le Mystere Des Psaumes.* Paris: Editions de L'Orante, 1954. A translation, by P. Fumaroli, of *Bread in the Wilderness.*

G29 *Saint Bernard de Clairvaux.* Paris: Editions D'Histoire et D'Art, Librairie Plon, 1954. A translation, by Daniel de Maupeou, O.S.B., of *The Last of the Fathers.*

G30 *L'Exil S'Acheve dans la Gloire.* Paris: Desclee de Brouwer, 1955. A translation, by a Carmelite Nun, of *Exile Ends in Glory.* [With a Preface by M. Gabriel Sortais, and a new Introduction by Thomas Merton.]

G31 *Le Signe de Jonas.* Paris: Editions Albin Michel, 1955. A translation, by Marie Tadie, of *The Sign of Jonas.*

G32 *Nul N'Est une Ile.* Paris: Aux Editions du Seuil, 1956. A translation, by Marie Tadie, of *No Man Is an Island.*

G33 *Le Pain Vivant.* Paris: Alsatia, 1957. A translation, by Marie Tadie, of *The Living Bread.*

G34 *La Vie Silencieuse.* Paris: Aux Editions du Seuil, 1958. A translation, by Marie Tadie, of *The Silent Life.*

G35 *Prions les Psaumes.* Paris: Editions du Cloitre, 1959. A translation, by Carmen Bernos de Gasztold, of *Praying the Psalms.*

G36 *La Paix Monastique.* Paris: Editions Albin Michel, 1962. A translation, by Marie Tadie, of *Monastic Peace.*

G37 *Direction Spirituelle et Meditation.* Paris: Editions Albin Michel, 1962. A translation, by Marie Tadie, of *Spiritual Direction and Meditation.*

G38 *Nouvelles Semences de Contemplation.* Paris: Aux Editions du Seuil, 1964. A translation, by Marie Tadie, of *New Seeds of Contemplation.*

G39 *Journal d'un Laic.* Paris: Editions Albin Michel, 1964. A translation, by Marie Tadie, of *The Secular Journal of Thomas Merton.*

G40 *La Revolution Noire* (excerpt: *Seeds of Destruction*). Paris: Castermann, 1964. Trans. Marie Tadie.

G41 *Semences de Destruction.* Paris: Editions Albin Michel, 1965. A translation, by Marie Tadie, of *Seeds of Destruction.*

G42 *Vie et Saintete.* Paris: Aux Editions du Seuil, 1966. A translation, by Marie Tadie, of *Life and Holiness.*

G43 *La Sagesse du Desert.* Paris: Editions Albin Michel, 1967. A translation, by Marie Tadie, of *The Wisdom of the Desert.*

G44 *Le Nouvel Homme.* Paris: Editions du Seuil, 1969. A translation, by Marie Tadie, of *The New Man.*

G45 *Foi et Violence.* Paris: Editions de l'Epi, 1969. A translation, by Marie Tadie, of *Faith and Violence.*

G46 *Le Temps des Fetes.* Paris: Castermann, 1969. A translation, by Marie Tadie, of *Seasons of Celebration.*

G47 *Reflexions d'un Spectateur Coupable.* Paris: Editions Albin Michel, 1970. A translation, by Marie Tadie, of *Conjectures of a Guilty Bystander.*

GERMAN

G48 *Der Berg der Sieben Stufen.* Zurich: Benziger Verlag, 1950. A translation, by Hans Grossrieder, of *The Seven Storey Mountain.*

G49 *Verheissungen der Stille.* Luzern: Raber-Verlag, 1951. A translation, by Magda Larsen, of *Seeds of Contemplation.*

G50 *Der Aufstieg zur Wahrheit.* Zurich: Benziger Verlag, 1952. A translation, by Hans Grossrieder, of *The Ascent to Truth.*

G51 *Von der Verbannung zur Herrlichkeit.* Luzern: Rex-Verlag, 1953. A translation, by Irene Marinoff, of *Exile Ends in Glory.*

G52 *Auserwahlt zu Leid und Wonne.* Luzern: Raber-Verlag, 1953. A translation, by Pater Sales Hess, of *What Are These Wounds?* [Contains a Preface by the translator, and an Introduction by Dr. Leddegar Hunkeler.]

G53 *Das Zeichen des Jonas.* Zurich: Benziger Verlag, 1954.
A translation, by Annemarie von Puttkamer, of
The Sign of Jonas.

G54 *Brot in der Wuste.* Zurich: Benziger Verlag, 1955. A
translation, by Annemarie von Puttkamer, of *Bread in
the Wilderness.*

G55 *Vom Sinn der Kontemplation.* Zurich: Verlag der Arche,
1955. A translation, by Alfred Kuoni, of *What Is
Contemplation?*

G56 *Keiner ist eine Insel.* Zurich: Benziger Verlag, 1956. A
translation, by Annemarie von Puttkamer, of *No Man
Is An Island.*

G57 *Schweigen im Himmel.* Wiesbaden: Verl-Anst, 1957.
A translation, by Erna Melchers, of *Silence in Heaven.*

G58 *Apokalypse der Neuen Welt.* Zurich: Verlag der Arche,
1957. A translation, by Alfred Kuoni, of *Figures for
an Apocalypse.*

G59 *Der mit dir Lebt.* Köln: Benziger, 1958. A translation,
by Irene Marinoff, of *The Living Bread.*

G60 *Der mit dir Lebt.* Zurich: Benziger, 1958. A translation,
by Irene Marinoff, of *The Living Bread.*

G61 *Lebendige Stille.* Köln: Benziger, 1959. A translation, by
Irene Marinoff, of *The Silent Life.*

G62 *Weltliches Tagebuch.* Köli: Benziger, 1960. A translation,
by Alfred Kuoni, of *The Secular Journal of Thomas
Merton.*

G63 *Verheissungen der Stille.* Luzern: Raber-Verlag, 1963.
A translation, by Magda Larsen and Paul F. Portmann, of
New Seeds of Contemplation.

G64 *Heilig in Christus.* Freiburg i. Br.: Herder, 1964. A
translation, by Eugen Kende, of *Life and Holiness.*

G65 *Die Schwarze Revolution* (excerpt: *Seeds of Destruction*).
Freiburg i. Br.: Herder, 1965. Trans. Hans Schmidthus.

G66 *Grazias Haus.* Einsiedeln: Johannes Verlag, 1966. A
translation, by Marta Gisi & Lili Sertorius, of *Selected
Poems of Thomas Merton & Emblems of a Season of Fury.*

GREEK

G67 *Exomologeseis Tou Anthropou Tou Eikostou Aionos.*
Athenai: "Tenos", 1969. This pamphlet contains excerpts
from Merton's following books: *Thirty Poems, The
Seven Storey Mountain, The Tears of the Blind Lions, No
Man Is An Island, Basic Principles of Monastic Spirituality,
Life and Holiness, Seeds of Destruction, Conjectures of a
Guilty Bystander,* a brief letter dated 9 November 1968,
and on back cover: a short extract from *Conjectures of a
Guilty Bystander.* Translated by E. Karita.

G68 *O Kainourgios Anthropos.* Athenai: Kalos Typos, 1971.
A translation, by Antonios Bakondios, of *The New Man.*

ITALIAN

G69 *La Montagna delle Sette Balze.* Milano: Garzanti, 1950.
A translation, by Alberto Castelli, of *The Seven Storey
Mountain.*

G70 *Poesie* [a pamphlet; a collection of poems]. Brescia:
Morcelliana, 1950. Translator: Augusto Guidi. [The verses
assembled here are: "La fuga in Egitto," "La Vite," "La

sera della Visitazione," "Sera," "Il Santissimo sull'altare,"
"Le donne greche," "La processione della Candelora,"
"Cana," "Trappisti al lavoro," "Invocazione a Santa
Lucia," "S. Tommaso d'Aquino," "La biografia," "Canto
per il Santissimo Sacramento," "Chiaravalle."]

G71 *La Poesia e la Vita Contemplativa* [a pamphlet]. Brescia:
Morcelliana, 1950. A translation, by Augusto Guidi, of
the Essay: *Poetry and the Contemplative Life*; see A5,
B3, C14.

G72 *Semi di Contemplazione.* Milano: Garzanti, 1951. A
translation, by Bruno Tasso, of *Seeds of Contemplation.*

G73 *Le Acque di Siloe.* Milano: Garzanti, 1951. A translation,
by Bruno Tasso, of *The Waters of Siloe.*

G74 *Che Cosa e la Contemplazione* [pamphlet]. Brescia:
Morcelliana, 1951. A translation, by Maddalena De Luca,
of *What Is Contemplation?*

G75 *Che Sono Queste Ferite?* Milano: Garzanti, 1952. A
translation, by Cecilia Tirone, of *What Are These Wounds?*

G76 *L'Esilio e la Gloria.* Brescia: Morcelliana, 1952. A
translation, by P. Giorgia Tansini, of *Exile Ends in Glory.*
[Contains an Introduction by the translator.]

G77 *Il Segno di Giona.* Milano: Garzanti, 1953. A translation,
by P. Silvio Zarattini, S.J., of *The Sign of Jonas.*

G78 *Un'Equilibrata Vita di Preghiera* [a pamphlet]. Brescia:
Morcelliana, 1953. A translation, by Maddalena De Luca, of
A Balanced Life of Prayer.

G79 *Ascesa alla Verita.* Milano: Garzanti, 1955. A translation,
by Cecilia Tirone, of *The Ascent to Truth.* [Contains
a Preface by P. Arcadio Larraona, C.M.F.]

G80 *Nessun Uomo e Un'Isola.* Milano: Garzanti, 1956. A translation, by Emanuela Moretti, of *No Man Is An Island.*

G81 *Vita nel Silenzio.* Brescia: Morcelliana, 1957. A translation, by M. R. Cimnaghi, of *The Silent Life.*

G82 *Il Pane nel Deserto.* Milano: Garzanti, 1958. A translation, of *Bread in the Wilderness.*

G83 *Il Pane Vivo.* Milano: Garzanti, 1958. A translation of *The Living Bread.*

G84 *Pensieri nella Solitudine.* Milano: Garzanti, 1960. A translation of *Thoughts in Solitude.*

G85 *I Salmi* [a pamphlet]. Vicenza: La locusta, 1961. A translation, by Rienzo Colla, of *Praying the Psalms.*

G86 *Diario Secolare.* Milano: Garzanti, 1961. A translation, by Lucia P. Rodocanachi, of *The Secular Journal of Thomas Merton.*

G87 *Pasternak* [a pamphlet; excerpt: *Disputed Questions*]. Vicenza: La locusta, 1962. Trans. Antonio Barbieri.

G88 *L'Uomo Nuovo.* Milano: Garzanti, 1963. A translation, by Franco Bernardini Marzolla, of *The New Man.*

G89 *Problemi dello Spirito.* Milano: Garzanti, 1964. A translation, by Franco Bernardini Marzolla, of *Disputed Questions.*

G90 *Vita e Santita.* Milano: Garzanti, 1964. A translation, by Franco Bernardini Marzolla, of *Life and Holiness.*

G91 *La Rivoluzione Negra* [a pamphlet] (excerpt: *Seeds of Destruction*). Vicenza, La locusta, 1965. Trans. Franco Onorati.

G92 *Nuovi Semi di Contemplazione.* Milano: Garzanti, 1965. A translation, by Bruno Tasso & Elena L. Rospigliosi, of *New Seeds of Contemplation.*

G93 *Direzione Spirituale e Meditazione.* Milano: Garzanti, 1965. A translation, by Elena L. Rospigliosi, of *Spiritual Direction and Meditation.*

G94 *Semi di Distruzione.* Milano: Garzanti, 1966. A translation, by Franco Bernardini Marzolla, of *Seeds of Destruction.*

G95 *Fede e Violenza.* Brescia: Morcelliana, 1966. A translation, by M. T. D'Agliano, of *Faith and Violence.*

G96 *Tempo di Celebrazione.* Milano: Garzanti, 1967. A translation, by Gino Rampini, of *Seasons of Celebration.*

G97 *Diario di un Testimone Colpevole.* Milano: Garzanti, 1969. A translation, by Gino Rampini, of *Conjectures of a Guilty Bystander.*

G98 *Fede Resistenza Protesta.* Brescia: Morcelliana, 1969. A translation, by M. T. D'Agliano, of *Faith and Violence* (original title: *Fede e Violenza;* see G95).

G99 *Hora Sedmi Stupnuu* [Ces.]. Rim, Krest'anska akademie, 1970. A translation of *The Seven Storey Mountain.*

G100 *Mistici e Maestri Zen.* Milano: Garzanti, 1970. A translation, by Franco Bernardini Marzolla, of *Mystics and Zen Masters.*

G101. *Lo Zen e gli Uccelli Rapaci.* Milano: Garzanti, 1970. A translation, by Franco Bernardini Marzolla, of *Zen and the Birds of Appetite.*

G102 *Il Clima della Preghiera Monastica.* Milano: Garzanti, 1970. A translation, by Franco Bernardini Marzolla, of *The Climate of Monastic Prayer.*

JAPANESE

G103 *Nanae No Yama.* Tokyo: Chuo shuppansha, 1966. A translation, by Kudo Tadashi, of *The Seven Storey Mountain.*

G104 *Meiso no Shushi.* Tokyo: Chuo shuppansha, 1966. A translation, by Nagasawa Junji, of *Seeds of Contemplation.*

KOREAN

G105 *Hyeondaeineui Sinang Saenghwal.* Seoul: Kaetoric Chulpansa, 1965. A translation, by Jeong-Jin Kim, of *Life and Holiness.*

POLISH

G106 *Nikt Nie Jest Samotna Wyspa.* Krakow: Znak, 1961. A translation, by Maria Morstin-Gorska, of *No Man Is An Island.*

G107 *Znak Jonasza.* Krakow: Znak, 1963. A translation, by Krystyna Poborska, of *The Sign of Jonas.*

PORTUGUESE

G108 *A Montanha dos Sete Patamares.* Rio de Janeiro: Editora Merito, 1952. A translation, by Jose Geraldo Vieira, of *The Seven Storey Mountain.*

G109 *O Signo de Jonas.* Rio de Janeiro: Editora Merito, 1954.
A translation, by Jose Geraldo Vieira, of *The Sign of
Jonas.*

G110 *Sementes de Contemplacao.* Porto: Livraria Tavares
Martins, 1955. A translation, by Teresa Leitao de Barros,
of *Seeds of Contemplation.*

G111 *Noite Sem Estrellas.* Lisboa: Bertrant, 1958. A
translation, by Susana Vasques, of *The Seven Storey
Mountain.*

G112 *Aguas de Siloe.* Belo Horizonte: Editora Itatiaia,
Limitada, 1958. A translation, by Oscar Mendes,
of *The Waters of Siloe.*

G113 *Homem Algum e Uma Ilha.* Rio de Janeiro, Agir, 1958.
A translation, by D. Timoteo Amorose Anastacio,
O.S.B., of *No Man Is An Island.*

G114 *Bernardo de Claraval.* Petropolis: Vozes, 1959.
A translation of *The Last of the Fathers.*

G115 *O Pao Vivo.* Petropolis: Vozes, 1960. A translation
of *The Living Bread.*

G116 *Diario Secular.* Petropolis: Vozes, 1961. A translation,
by Alceu Amoroso Lima, of *The Secular Journal
of Thomas Merton.*

G117 *A Vida Silenciosa.* Petropolis: Vozes, 1961. A
translation of the *Silent Life.*

G118 *Direcao Espiritual e Meditacao.* Petropolis: Vozes, 1963.
A translation of *Spiritual Direction and Meditation.*

G119 *Novas Sementes de Contemplacao.* Petropolis: Vozes,
1963. A translation of *New Seeds of Contemplation.*

G120 *Questoes Abertas*. Rio de Janeiro: Liv. Agir, 1963. A translation of *Disputed Questions*.

G121 *O Pao no Deserto*. Petropolis: Vozes, 1964. A translation of *Bread in the Wilderness*.

G122 *Vida e Santidade*. S. Paulo: Herder, 1965. A translation of *Life and Holiness*.

G123 *O Homem Novo*. Guanabara: Agir, 1967. A translation of *The New Man*.

G124 *A Via de Chuang Tzu*. Petropolis: Vozes, 1969. A translation, by Paulo Alceu Amoroso Lima, of *The Way of Chuang Tzu*.

G125 *Vinho do Silencio* [a pamphlet; a collection of poems]. Belo Horizonte: Imprensa da Universidade Federal de Minas Gerais, 1969. Translated by Carmen de Mello.

G126 *Zen e as Aves de Rapina*. Brazil: Editora Civilizacao Brasileira, 1972. A translation of *Zen and the Birds of Appetite*.

SPANISH

G127 *La Montana de los Siete Circulos*. Buenos Aires: Editorial Sudamericana, 1950. A translation, by Aquilino Tur, of *The Seven Storey Mountain*.

G128 *Semillas de Contemplacion*. Buenos Aires: Editorial Sudamericana, 1952. A translation, by C. A. Jordana, of *Seeds of Contemplation*.

G129 *Las Aguas de Siloe*. Buenos Aires: Editorial Sudamericana, 1952. A translation, by Maria de Los Dolores Amores Jimenez, of *The Waters of Siloe*.

G130 *Veinte Poemas* [a pamphlet; a collection of poems]. Madrid: Ediciones Rialp, 1953. Translated and with an Introduction by Jose Maria Valverde.

G131 *Ascenso a la Verdad*. Buenos Aires: Editorial Sudamericana, 1954. A translation, by Alberto Luis Bixio, of *The Ascent to Truth*.

G132 *El Signo de Jonas*. Mexico: Editorial Cumbre, 1954. A translation, by Julio Fernandez Yanez, of *The Sign of Jonas*.

G133 *La Senda de la Contemplacion* [a pamphlet; a collection of essays]. Madrid: Ediciones Rialp, 1955. A translation, by Antonio Ugalde y Mariano del Pozo, of *La Renuncia y el Cristiano* (see C44), *Un Vida de Oracion Equilibrada* (see A14), *Que Es La Contemplacion?* (see A8, G74), *Poesia y Vida Contemplativa* (see A5, B3, C14, G71).

G134 *Pan en el Desierto*. Buenos Aires: Editorial Sudamericana, 1955. A translation, by Gonzalo Meneses Ocon, of *Bread in the Wilderness*.

G135 *El Signo de Jonas*. Barcelona, Exito, 1955. A translation, by Julio Fernandez Yanez, of *The Sign of Jonas*.

G136 *San Bernardo, El Ultimo de los Padres*. Madrid: Ediciones Rialp, 1956. A translation, by Father Victorio Peral, of *The Last of the Fathers*.

G137 *Los Hombres no son Islas*. Buenos Aires: Editorial Sudamericana, 1956. A translation, by Gonzalo Meneses Ocon, of *No Man Is An Island*.

G138 *El Pan Vivo*. Madrid: Ediciones Rialp, 1957. A translation of *The Living Bread*.

G139 *La Vida Silenciosa.* Buenos Aires: Editorial Sudamericana, 1958. A translation, by Maria Josefina Martinez Alinari, of *The Silent Life.*

G140 *Pensamientos de la Soledad.* Buenos Aires: Editorial Sudamericana, 1960. A translation, by Maria Josefina Martinez Alinari, of *Thoughts in Solitude.*

G141 *Poemas* [a pamphlet; a collection of poems]. Mexico: UNAM, 1961. Trans. Ernesto Cardenal.

G142 *El Exilio y la Gloria.* Buenos Aires: Editorial Sudamericana, 1961. A translation, by Aquilino Tur, of *Exile Ends in Glory.*

G143 *Cuestiones Discutidas.* Barcelona: EDHASA, 1962. A translation, by Maria Josefina Martinez Alinari, of *Disputed Questions.*

G144 *Cuestiones Discutidas.* Buenos Aires: Editorial Sudamericana, 1962. A translation, by Juana Martinez Alinari, of *Disputed Questions.*

G145 *Nuevas Semillas de Contemplacion.* Buenos Aires: Editorial Sudamericana, 1964. A translation, by Maria Josefina Martinez Alinari, of *New Seeds of Contemplation.*

G146 *Vida I Santedat* [Cat.]. Barcelona: Herder, 1965. A translation of *Life and Holiness.*

G147 *La Revolucio Negra* [Cat.] (excerpt: *Seeds of Destruction*). Barcelona: Estela, 1965. Trans. by Jose Verde Aldea.

G148 *La Revolucion Negra* (excerpt: *Seeds of Destruction*). Barcelona: Estela, 1965. Trans. Angeles Maragall.

179

G149 *Ningu no es una Illa* [Cat.]. Barcelona, Edicions, 1966.
A translation, by Herminia Grau de Duran, of
No Man Is An Island.

G150 *Semillas de Destruccion*. Barcelona: Pomaire, 1966.
A translation, by Jose Maria Valverde, of *Seeds of
Destruction*.

G151 *Tiempos de Celebracion*. Barcelona: Pomaire, 1967.
A translation, by Jose Maria Valverde, of *Seasons
of Celebration*.

G152 *El Hombre Nuevo*. Barcelona: Pomaire, 1967. A
translation, by Jose Maria Valverde, of *The New Man*.

G153 *Conjeturas de un Espectador Culpable*. Barcelona:
Pomaire, 1967. A translation, by Jose Maria Valverde,
of *Conjectures of a Guilty Bystander*.

G154 *El Exilio y la Gloria*. Barcelona: Pomaire, 1969. A
translation, by Maria Espineira, of *Exile Ends in Glory*.

SWEDISH

G155 *Vagen till Kontemplation*. Stockholm: Petrus de
Dacia-Forlag, 1954. A translation, by Fil Dr. Daniel
Andreae, of *Seeds of Contemplation*.

G156 *Kallad till Tystnad*. Lund: Gleerupska Univ. Bokh, 1956.
A translation, by M. & S. Stolpe, of *The Seven Storey
Mountain*.

G157 *Den Heliga Tystnaden*. Malmo: Allhem, 1956. A
translation, by Erik Cinthio, of *Silence in Heaven*.

G158 *Brod i Odemarken*. Stockholm: Petrus de Dacia, 1959. A translation, by Marianne Pauchard & Kajsa Rottzen, of *Bread in the Wilderness*.

VIETNAMESE

G159 *Hat Giong Chiem Niem*. Saigon: Phong Trao Van Hoa, 1966. A translation, by Thanh Bang, of *Seeds of Contemplation*.

H. Juvenilia Contributions by Thomas Merton to School Publications

Arranged chronologically

The following abbreviations are used: CJ (The Columbia Jester); CR (The Columbia Review), and CS (The Columbia Spectator).

H1 Editorial; "An Unfortunate Oakhamian" [black and white cartoon drawn by author accompanies article]; "Motlie Notis" [minus the poem, which was by someone else]; "The City Without a Soul" [title and some of the remarks were dictated by the Moderator of the Magazine!]. *The Oakhamian*, XLVII (Christmas Term 1931) [1], 18, 19, 23-24.

H2 Editorial; "Society Notes"; "Strasbourg Cathedral"; "The New Boy Who Won Through"; "Lines to a Crafty Septuagenarian" [a poem]; "On the Musical Propensities of VI Classical" [a poem]; "Answers to Correspondents." *The Oakhamian*, XLVII (Easter Term 1932) [1], 16-18, 18, 21-22, 24, 27, 28.

H3 Editorial; "Dies Orationum" [a poem]; "Wahlt Hitler." *The Oakhamian*, XLVII (Summer Term 1932) [1], 25, 29-30.

H4 Editorial; "The Passing of Sir Lafournayse"; "Fragment
of Roman Bas-relief" [black and white cartoon drawn
by author accompanies article];"Certificate Y"; "A Classical
Ditty" [a poem]. *The Oakhamian*, XLVIII (Christmas
Term 1932) [1], 22, 23, 25-26, 26.

H5 "Paris in Chicago." *The Granta*, XLIII. 971 (November
29, 1933) 144.

H6 "A Crust for Egoists." *The Granta*, XLIII. 981
(April 25, 1934) 355.

H7 [A letter to] *Esquire*, II. 6 (November, 1934) 14.

H8 "Katabolism of an Englishman." *CJ*, XXVI. 1
(September, 1935) 12, plus 28.

H9 "Suburban Demon." *CJ*, XXVI. 3 (November, 1935) 7.

H10 "At the Corner." *CR*, XVII. 1 (November, 1935) 8.

H11 "The More Abundant Life"; "Students Awake." *CJ*,
XXVI. 4 (December, 1935) 14, 15, plus 39.

H12 "The Chaste." *CJ*, XXVI. 5 (January, 1936) 18, plus 22.

H13 "Springtime for Webster." *CJ*, XXVI. 6
(February, 1936) 15.

H14 "Success Story." *CJ*, XXVI. 7 (March, 1936) 12, plus 33.

H15 "Chorines vs. Ponies: Who Wins?" *CS*, LIX. 100
(March 18, 1936) 1:3.

H16 "Bob Burke Loses Jinx Fight on Technical K.O. in
Garden." *CS*, LIX. 104 (March 24, 1936) 1:2, plus 3:2.

H17 "Burke's Shoulder Old-Time Jinx." *CS*, LIX. 105
(March 25, 1936) 3:5.

H18 "Spring Gets Jester Editors"; "Boys Plan Barnard Section."
CS, LIX. 114 (April 7, 1936) 1:2.

H19 [A column; "The Off-Hour."] *CS*, LIX. 118
(April 16, 1936) 2:2.

H20 [A column; "The Stroller."] *CS*, LIX. 124
(April 24, 1936) 2.2.

H21 "Napoleon or Something." *CJ*, XXVI. 9
(May, 1936) 11-12.

H22 [A column; "The Off-Hour."] *CS*, LIX. 130
(May 4, 1936) 2:2.

H23 [A column; "The Stroller."] *CS*, LIX. 135
(May 11, 1936) 2:3.

H24 "They Grow in September"; "The Best Things in Life";
"Your Night to Howl." *CJ*, XXXVII: 1 (September, 1936)
12, 14, 16-19.

H25 [An untitled story about the Observation Roofs which
was included in the column:] "What Goes On."
Rockefeller Center Weekly, 5. 10 (September 4, 1936) 13.
(Defunct.)

H26 "Did the Reds Get Evander Crotch?" *CJ*, XXXVII. 2
(October, 1936) 28-31.

H27 [A column; "The Stroller."] *CS*, LX. 17
(October 16, 1936) 2:2.

H28 "Latins are Lousy Pornographers"; "Concerning
Tennyson McGap." *CJ*, XXXVII. 3 (November, 1936)
14-15, 18.

H29 "How Time Goes"; "Your Night to Howl." *CJ*,
XXXVIII. 4 (December, 1936) 26-27, 32-33.

H30 [A column; "The Stroller."] *CS*, LX. 91
(March 11, 1937). 2:2.

H31 "Raw Lie Unraw" [first line of untitled poem]. *CJ*,
XXXIX. 2 (October, 1937) 16.

H32 "Mr. and Mrs. Jim Huttner." *CR*, XIX. 1
(November, 1937) 8-13.

H33 'Nineteen Questions for Social Blights." *CJ*, XXXIX. 3
(November, 1937) 24.

H34 "Happy Planets, Happy Beasts" [a poem]. *CJ*. XXXIX.
4 (December, 1937) 16.

H35 "Old Glory, Old Junk." *CJ*, XXXIX. 5 (January, 1938)
8, plus 23.

H36 "Window" [a poem]; "Voyage to Nyack"; "Your Night
to Howl." *CJ*, XXXIX. 7 (March, 1938) 10, 12, plus 26, 21.

H37 "Huxley and the Ethics of Peace." *CR*, XIX. 2
(March, 1938) 13-18.

H38 "Look, Tiger"; "Spring for All" [poems]. *CJ*, XXXIX. 8
(April, 1938) 33.

H39 "Bureaucrats: Diggers" [a poem; see F1]. *CR*, XIX. 3
(Summer 1938) 13.

H40 "Anatomy of Journals." *CJ*, XXXIX. 9 (May, 1938)
10, plus 28.

H41 "Fourth Discourse Concerning the Elephant"; "Pastoral
for Maytime" [a poem]; "Legends are all Lies." *CJ*,
XXXIX. 10 (June, 1938) 7, 14, 18-19.

H42 "Oasis: A Crust for the Frosh." *CJ*, XL. 1
(September, 1938) 21, plus 29.

H43 "Oasis: M. A. Thesis"; "Woods are not Sober" [first line
of untitled poem]. *CJ*, XL. 2 (October, 1938) 16, 24.

H44 "High Life: Sleep"; "Martians." *CJ*, XL. 3
(November, 1938) 10-11, 13.

H45 "Two Things for Christmas" [a poem]; [A review of]
Garland of Bays. By Gwyn Jones. *CJ*, XL. 4
(December, 1938) 14, 27.

H46 "Fable of Heriger." *CJ*, XL. 6 (February, 1939) 11.

H47 "Concerning Tennyson McGap." *CJ*, XL. 9 (May, 1939)
7.

H48 "The Question of the Beard." *CJ*, C. 1 (September, 1939)
10-11.

H49 "Masque of Melancholy." *CJ*, C. 2 (October, 1939) 20-21.

H50 "The Art of Richard Hughes." *CR*, XXI. 1
(November, 1939) 13-18.

H51 "Fable: The Profiteer," by F. Xavier Sheridan [Merton's
nom de plume]. *CJ*, C. 4 (December, 1939) 6-7.

H52 "The Beetle Becomes the Prince of Creatures and Makes a
Choice" (an opera), by F. X. Sheridan [to my knowledge,
these are the only two instances where Father Louis has
used a pseudonym]. *CJ*, C. 8 (April, 1940) 24-26.

Indexes

Book Index

Index of Merton Articles

Poetry Index

204

Index of Foreign Publications

208

210

Index of Translators

Index of Juvenilia

Index of Names

215

Thornton, Francis B., F35
Thornton, Martin, C229
Tillyard, E. M. W., C8
Tindall, William York, C11
Tobin, James E., B8, F62
Towne, Charles Hanson, F1
Traherne, T., C158
Turbessi, Giuseppe, C257
Turner, Nat, C364
Tzu, Chuang, A43, C362a

Underhill, Evelyn, C242

Van Doren, Charles, B21, F63
Van Doren, Mark, A32, F51, F53
Versfeld, Martin, C272
Vitale, Philip, B42a

Walley, Dean, A54
Walsh, Richard J., A26
Warren, Robert Penn, C315

Waugh, Evelyn, C33, E1
Weil, Simone, C251
Wenzel, S., C354, C412
White, Helen C., F12
Wienpahl, Paul, C242
Wilder, Amos N., F57
Williams, George H., C308
Williams, Margaret A., E17
Woods, Ralph L., B13, B18, F49
Woolf, Cecil, B57
Wu, J. C., B60

Zahn, Gordon C., A60, C245, C254a
Zander, Vera, C293
Zanders, J. W., A26
Zapf, Hermann, A54
Zaturenska, Marya, F71
Zeitz, Gray, E17
Zukofsky, Louis, C311a, C323
Zwang, Theophil, A26